Dec 1997

To Bill

from Sharon

ROUND RIVER

ROUND RIVER

From the Journals of Aldo Leopold

Edited by Luna B. Leopold

Illustrated by Charles W. Schwartz

OXFORD UNIVERSITY PRESS
Oxford · *New York*

Oxford University Press

Oxford   New York   Toronto
Delhi   Bombay   Calcutta   Madras   Karachi
Kuala Lumpur   Singapore   Hong Kong   Tokyo
Nairobi   Dar es Salaam   Cape Town
Melbourne   Auckland   Madrid

and associated companies in
Berlin   Ibadan

Library of Congress Cataloging-in-Publication Data
Leopold, Aldo, 1886–1948.
Round River ; from the journals of Aldo Leopold / edited by Luna
B. Leopold ; illustrated by Charles W. Schwartz.
p.   cm.
ISBN 0-19-501563-0
1. Leopold, Aldo, 1886–1948—Diaries.   2. Naturalists—Wisconsin—
Diaries.   3. Natural history—North America—Outdoor books.
I. Leopold, Luna Bergere, 1915–   .   II. Title.
QH31.L618A3   1993   799'.092—dc20   93-9159   CIP

4 6 8 10 9 7 5 3

Printed in the United States of America

To
Fritz, Bruce, Ninita, Wendy,
and the others
for they will become navigators
on the Round River

Preface

'I know an island that is too sandy to make a field and too brushy to make a pasture; a shining river divides to wash its shores, and to hold a mirror to its tall birches. In summer mosquitoes and poison ivy defend its shores against the fisherman; in winter treacherous ice and wide bars fence out the woodcutter.

'My island has no name, for no one has ever died, fought, camped, or farmed there to give it one. History has passed it by.

'So did I, until one day I noticed the extraordinary number of deer tracks crossing the wide bar to the only ford. If the deer like to go there, I thought, I had better take a look. I have often noticed that a deer's taste in scenery and solitudes is very much like my own.

'Years ago the title to my island bounced back to the county, where it has reposed very quietly ever since. The county holds it in trust, as it were, for the deer and myself. The peculiarity of this arrangement is that the county knows nothing about it.'

In these words Aldo Leopold described one of his greatest possessions. It ranked with the old horse's skull on the fence post, reclaimed from complete dismemberment by virtue of some rusty baling wire, but which could be counted on to conceal a brood of bluebirds every spring. It ranked with the tree-house in the elm, from which gay laughter and guitar music could be heard during every school holiday. There were the pasque flowers on the sandhill, the wahoo bushes to which the rabbits claimed proprietory rights, the splash of fall yellow in the hickories of the distant hills.

Value is not measured entirely by scarcity, and possession may have a little to do with the law. But to be rich in these subtle goods requires a perception that grows slowly and sometimes not at all.

Perception is not acquired by formal education, nor is it necessarily vouchsafed to those who are learned in the arts or sciences. Perception is merely a recognition of ethical and aesthetic values to be found in natural things. It is clear, therefore, that perception is something that grows through various stages of development.

Aldo Leopold's journals provide some hint of the progress of this development. The journal entries included in the present volume will indicate the source of some of the ideas on land ethics represented by his essays. Some of the essays are sampled here and others comprised a previous volume, *A Sand County Almanac*.

The present volume is keynoted by an opening essay on 'A Man's Leisure Time.' It is followed by excerpts from his journals which show in more direct form what he did with his own leisure. These excerpts constitute only a few of hundreds of journal entries, most of them shorter than those included here.

Most of the journal notes included in the second part of this book were written around a campfire. They have, I think, some of the pungency of oak smoke; the original pages are here and there spattered with a slapped mosquito or a drop of camp coffee. They convey some measure of insight into the camp and field experience from which perception gradually emerged.

The essays separating some of the journal entries and making up the final part of this book are taken from more contemplative notes which were in the form of unfinished manuscripts when Aldo died. These resulted from a lifetime of developing perception. They express in words the feelings of a large number of people less gifted than he in writing, but whose sense of values is similar. For those of us less gifted, our experiences can be mirrored in his words.

Luna B. Leopold

Washington, D. C.
July 1953

Dramatis Personae

The entries in Aldo Leopold's journals usually began with notes on locale, weather, and dates in the upper right corner of the page. In the upper left were initials of the members of the party. On long trips some of the daily journal entries were made by other members of the family. At the beginning of each such entry, the editor has inserted in parentheses initials that will serve to identify the author of that portion.

        E.B.L.   Estella B. Leopold (Mother)

The Leopold children
        A.S.L.   A. Starker Leopold
        L.B.L.   Luna B. Leopold
        A.M.L. Adelina M. Leopold
        A.C.L. A. Carl Leopold
        E.L.   Estella Leopold

Aldo Leopold's brothers
        C.S.L. Carl S. Leopold
        F.L.   Frederic Leopold

FLICK—Nearly any and all dogs in the Leopold family; in sequence; 1920–30, an English Setter; 1930–34, a Springer Spaniel;
GUS—A German Short-haired Pointer, 1935–43.

Contents

Part I

A MAN'S LEISURE TIME

A Man's Leisure Time

The text of this sermon is taken from the gospel according to Ariosto. I do not know the chapter and verse, but this is what he says: 'How miserable are the idle hours of the ignorant man!'

There are not many texts that I am able to accept as gospel truths, but this is one of them. I am willing to rise up and declare my belief that this text is literally true; true forward, true backward, true even before breakfast. The man who cannot enjoy his leisure is ignorant, though his degrees exhaust the alphabet, and the man who does enjoy his leisure is to some extent educated, though he has never seen the inside of a school.

I cannot easily imagine a greater fallacy than for one who has several hobbies to speak on the subject to those who may have none. For this implies prescription of avocation by one person for another, which is the antithesis of whatever virtue may inhere in having any at all. You do not annex a hobby, the hobby annexes you. To prescribe a hobby would be dangerously akin to prescribing a wife—with about the same probability of a happy outcome.

Let it be understood, then, that this is merely an exchange of reflections among those already obsessed—for better or for

3

worse—with the need of doing something queer. Let others listen if they will, and profit by our behavior if they can.

What is a hobby anyway? Where is the line of demarcation between hobbies and ordinary normal pursuits? I have been unable to answer this question to my own satisfaction. At first blush I am tempted to conclude that a satisfactory hobby must be in large degree useless, inefficient, laborious, or irrelevant. Certainly many of our most satisfying avocations today consist of making something by hand which machines can usually make more quickly and cheaply, and sometimes better. Nevertheless I must in fairness admit that in a different age the mere fashioning of a machine might have been an excellent hobby. Galileo, I fancy, derived a real and personal satisfaction when he set the ecclesiastical world on its ear by embodying in a new catapult some natural law that St. Peter had inadvertently omitted to catalogue. Today the invention of a new machine, however noteworthy to industry, would, as a hobby, be trite stuff. Perhaps we have here the real inwardness of our question: A hobby is a defiance of the contemporary. It is an assertion of those permanent values which the momentary eddies of social evolution have contravened or overlooked. If this is true, then we may also say that every hobbyist is inherently a radical, and that his tribe is inherently a minority.

This, however, is serious; becoming serious is a grievous fault in hobbyists. It is an axiom that no hobby should either seek or need rational justification. To wish to do it is reason enough. To find reasons why it is useful or beneficial converts it at once from an avocation into an industry—lowers it at once to the ignominious category of an 'exercise' undertaken for health, power, or profit. Lifting dumbbells is not a hobby. It is a confession of subservience, not an assertion of liberty.

When I was a boy, there was an old German merchant who

4

lived in a little cottage in our town. On Sundays he used to go out and knock chips off the limestone ledges along the Mississippi, and he had a great tonnage of these chips, all labeled and catalogued. The chips contained little fossil stems of some defunct water creatures called crinoids. The townspeople regarded this gentle old fellow as just a little bit abnormal, but harmless. One day the newspaper reported the arrival of certain titled strangers. It was whispered that these visitors were great scientists, some of them from foreign lands, and some were among the world's leading paleontologists. They came to visit the harmless old man, and to hear his pronouncements on crinoids, and they accepted these pronouncements as law. When the old German died, the town awoke to the fact that he was a world authority on his subject; a creator of knowledge; a maker of scientific history. He was a great man—a man beside whom the local captains of industry were mere bushwhackers. His collection went to a national museum, and his name is known in all the nations of the earth.

I knew a bank president who adventured in roses. Roses made him a happy man and a better bank president. I know a wheel manufacturer who adventures in tomatoes. He knows all about them, and, whether as a result or as a cause, he also knows all about wheels. I know a taxi driver who romances in sweet corn. Get him wound up once and you will be surprised how much he knows, and hardly less at how much there is to be known.

The most glamorous hobby I know of today is the revival of falconry. It has a few addicts in America, and perhaps a dozen in England—a minority indeed. For two and a half cents one can buy and shoot a cartridge that will kill the heron whose capture by hawking requires months or years of laborious training of both the hawk and the hawker. The cartridge, as a lethal agent, is a perfect product of industrial chemistry.

5

One can write a formula for its lethal reaction. The hawk, as a lethal agent, is the perfect flower of that still utterly mysterious alchemy—evolution. No living man can, or possibly ever will, understand the instinct of predation that we share with our raptorial servant. No man-made machine can, or ever

will, synthesize that perfect co-ordination of eye, muscle, and pinion as he stoops to his kill. The heron, if bagged, is inedible and hence useless (although the old falconers seem to have eaten him, just as a Boy Scout smokes and eats a flea-bitten summer cottontail that has fallen victim to his sling, club, or bow). Moreover the hawk, at the slightest error in technique of handling, may either 'go tame' like Homo sapiens or fly away into the blue. All in all falconry is the perfect hobby.

To make and shoot the longbow is another. There is a subversive belief among laymen that in the hands of an expert the bow is an efficient weapon. Each fall, less than a hundred Wisconsin experts register to hunt deer with the broadheaded arrow. One out of the hundred may get a buck, and he is surprised. One out of five riflemen gets his buck. As an archer, therefore, and on the basis of our record, I indignantly deny the allegation of efficiency. I admit only this: that making archery tackle is an effective alibi for being late at the office, or failing to carry out the ashcan on Thursdays.

One cannot make a gun—at least I can't. But I can make a bow, and some of them will shoot. And this reminds me that perhaps our definition ought to be amended; a good hobby, in these times, is one that entails either making something or making the tools to make it with, and then using it to accomplish some needless thing. When we have passed out of the present age, a good hobby will be the reverse of all these. I come again to the defiance of the contemporary.

A good hobby must also be a gamble. When I look at a rough, heavy, lumpy, splintery stave of *bois d'arc*, and envision the perfect gleaming weapon that will one day emerge from its graceless innards, and when I picture that bow, drawn in a perfect arc, ready—in a split second—to cleave the sky with its shining javelin, I must envision also the probability that it may—in a split second—burst into impotent splinters, while I

7

face another laborious month of evenings at the bench. The possible debacle is, in short, an essential element in all hobbies, and stands in bold contradistinction to the humdrum certainty that the endless belt will eventuate in a Ford.

A good hobby may be a solitary revolt against the commonplace, or it may be the joint conspiracy of a congenial group. That group may, on occasion, be the family. In either event it is a rebellion, and if a hopeless one, all the better. I cannot imagine a worse jumble than to have the whole body politic suddenly 'adopt' all the foolish ideas that smolder in happy discontent beneath the conventional surface of society. There is no such danger. Nonconformity is the highest evolutionary attainment of social animals, and will grow no faster than other new functions. Science is just beginning to discover what incredible regimentation prevails among the 'free' savages, and the freer mammals and birds. A hobby is perhaps creation's first denial of the 'peck-order' that burdens the gregarious universe, and of which the majority of mankind is still a part.

Part II

COUNTRY

The Delta Colorado

BEING AN ACCOUNT
OF A VOYAGE OF DISCOVERY
BY CARL AND ALDO LEOPOLD
GENTLEMEN—ADVENTURERS

In the Mythical Straits of Annian,
the Jungles of the Rio del Pescador,
and the Environs of the Vermillion Sea.
In the hunter's moon, A.D. 1922.

*Many voyages have been pretended, yet
hitherto never any thoroughly accomplished
by our nation, of exact discovery into the
bowels of those main, ample, and vast countries. . . .*

SIR HUMPHREY GILBERT

25 October, Wednesday

After arriving in Yuma at midnight Tuesday, we were up at daylight and found the river flowing under a bridge only a stone's throw from the hotel. It looked like plenty of water.

We called at Reclamation Service Headquarters, where I met Mr. Ray Priest, Assistant Project Manager. He had just been to the mouth of the river in a skiff with a traveler named Freeman, who had come down from the very headwaters. They had encountered three days' hard trucking in the Pescadero country, and Yuma had been about to send out a rescue party. Priest said not to try it. Mr. Berry of the Customs said the same.

We then went to see Colonel B. F. Fly, who very kindly devoted his whole day to seeing us off. After buying our chuck and getting haircuts, we left at 3 p.m. for San Luis in a Model T Ford truck belonging to Will Lowe. Having the canoe loaded on diagonally worked very well. An interesting ride through the rich Yuma Valley landed us at the International Boundary about 5 p.m. Here Colonel Fly introduced us to Major Y. Gomez Yavias, a government engineer, Alexandre Sorteon, our host for the night and driver for tomorrow, Major Arierza, the newly elected Comisario of San Luis, and Lieutenant Lopez, the commander of the garrison. It being agreed that we were harmless hunters and not the conspirators of a new revolution, we all repaired to the saloon and had some real beer. Colonel Fly then returned to Yuma, while we spent a very interesting evening at Sorteon's, discussing the country with Major Gomez and hearing always of the terrible tides or bores, and the impracticability of venturing into them with our canoe. It was finally decided to leave the canoe temporarily at San Luis while we spent a week or so at the head of the Rillito after deer.

Among the evening callers at Sorteon's was Señor Corvola, a finance inspector on a 'delicate mission,' the Comisario's office and records having been burned just a day or two before the recent election; also Señor Limon, government wireless operator.

Slept on the floor of Sorteon's restaurant, and awoke bright and early for the eventful *entrada*.

26 October, Thursday

Left about 10 a.m. in Sorteon's Ford for Rillito, where we arrived about 1 p.m. and unloaded on the bank of a pretty little slough, dismissing Sorteon with instructions to come back in a week. Even as we drove up to the slough a beautiful snowy heron flushed from the reedy bank, and several cormorants were fishing in a wide place below camp. Flick flushed a covey of quail.

We built an Apache style 'rancheria' for shade and after completing camp took a walk up the Rillito. Carl got one quail and we found an unbelievable number of bobcat and coyote tracks in the sandbars and on the banks of the stream. As we got back to camp a very large coyote was drinking just below at the head of the little lake—we nearly got a shot at him. That night we could hear geese passing—they would set up a great cackling when they saw our fire. Quite a coyote chorus during the night.

27 October, Friday

At daylight I killed a huge drake mallard flying up the stream. Explored upstream and got our first lesson in arrowweed thickets. They are barren deserts, full of unkillable but dog-killing rabbits, and travel is difficult to impossible. A couple of miles above camp we came on a very pretty lagoon, from which three widgeon flushed. Carl got them all. Here also were

12

the tracks of a huge buck and a doe. A great flock of wavies came exploring up the Rillito about 10 a.m. and went on back again—presumably to El Doctor. From the hill on the mesa near the lagoon we could see the whole delta and even the mirage—like mud flats at Santa Clara. A howling wilderness is the only name for it.

In the evening we set out a couple of traps above camp and tried the mullet, which were jumping in great numbers. No luck. Roast duck and sourdough biscuit tonight—but we spoiled the noodles by trying to boil them in the salty water from our 'well.'

At noon we had a swim and washday, likewise barbershop. Water fine but cold.

28 October, Saturday

Explored south. Deer tracks more numerous, including quite a few very small ones which may be fawns or maybe little white-tails. Rillito has many long pools, on which were snowy herons, night and great blue herons, cormorants, grebes, coots, and kingfishers. Also a few spoonbills. One flock of wavies came exploring upstream, and we heard another flock out on the mesa. More experience with arrowweed jungles.

There are a few cattle here, which seem to eat cane.

The quail killed yesterday had a crop full of berries, which we today identified as mistletoe. It grows on tornillo and mesquite.

About 2 p.m. heard an auto on the road. Carl went up. The two men in it didn't want to talk. They had the back seat full of wet-looking crates.

This evening we fished, Carl rigging a throwline. Got a big carp—probably two pounds—that fought at least as hard as a bass, several smaller carp, and a small mullet. Rabbit belly proved a better bait than pork fat.

At evening a team passed—a big burly Mexicano, four big mules, and probably a ton of 'hooch.' You could smell it *tambien*. The Mexicano proved to be Dominguez of La Bolsa. He camped at the 'Agua dulce' north of our camp and we fed him up on noodles and sourdough biscuits and then plied him in poor Spanish for information about deer and geese.

29 October, Sunday

A cold night. Some impertinent coon took our fish. The upper coyote trap had a drowned buzzard in it; the proverbial wet hen was handsome in comparison.

South along the mesa, quail hunting and prospecting. Got two birds, both full of tornillo hulls. A Gambel quail track is 2″ long x 1½″ wide toe to toe. There are five feathers in his plume.

On climbing one of the dunes, or 'montes,' we found a huge bay of low country south of camp and cut across to it. No deer tracks there or along the edge coming back. The deer must use the other montes east of camp.

Back at noon. After dinner a flock of avocets came over.

14

Carl got three. They are the most delicately beautiful of all waterbirds. Carl also killed one of the stout-billed waders that had a white rump; turned out to be a willet.

The rest of the afternoon we fished, catching many small mullet. Put them in a sandbar pool. Sunday dinner we had before dark by way of celebration—quail and mashed potatoes and a very successful batch of sourdough bread of which Carolo was the author—his first attempt.

30 October, Monday

As we were eating breakfast I knocked down a big mallard and Carolo two widgeons. Many geese flew up over the mesa and clamored mightily around the upper lagoon. We first went up to look at the traps. The first one was gone, and a clawed-up bank told us why. We were rather blankly wondering whether the light stake had come off when we heard a rustling back in the arrowweed. We broke our way through the dense growth, one to each side of the noise, and Carl sang out, 'Coyote!' and at the same time the coyote made a run for it. He made pretty good progress and we were afraid he might pull out. So Carl put a .32 bullet behind his ear and we carried our catch back to the Rillito. It was a very pretty young female in fine fur, but when we hung her up for skinning we found the fur was loose. So we had to content ourselves with the brush. So far it was a pretty large morning.

Then took a hike to the 'montes' north of camp but found no deer sign. When we got back at noon a blue heron was in our fish pen, and left with great reluctance and protestation.

The flats north of camp have many snail shells—evidently carried by high water.

Fished in the evening. Decided that our so-called 'carp' were sheepshead, as the mouth is not pointed downward, but forward, and they lack the carp's 'whiskers.'

15

Had sheepshead and mullet for supper, but found both were so soft and soapy as to be inedible.

The geese made a great to-do up the Rillito. Carl said it sounded like a daughter getting home from college.

Gathered up our traps preparatory to moving to the Punta de Mesa tomorrow, where there are said to be 'muchos venados.'

31 October, Tuesday

Francisco, a vaquero for Jesus of the Rancho Salado, arrived about 9 a.m. with his 'carrillo' and a team of buckskin mules. We loaded up and arrived at the Punta about noon, telling Francisco to come back Thursday.

Took a walk up the Colorado Viejo and set a trap with the carcass of a mallard. At the foot of the Punta are a series of pools, full of herons and lined with waving willows of the most delicate green; the water, bearing the reflections of the willows, is of a brilliant verdigris hue. A weird and impressive place. No deer tracks. Killed four quail. Their crops contained a few tornillo hulls and whole grasshoppers, and a huge amount of minute, hard, lozenge-shaped, shiny, bronze-black seed, together with the hulls. I think this must be pigweed (arrowweed) seed. They contain a white kernel.

A very pleasant camp on the mesa in a clump of mesquite trees. Had the mallard for supper, with whole rice. (At the Rillito camp a coyote got away with our trap—pulled the stake.)

1 November, Wednesday

Down the Rillito. Found some deer tracks, most of them old, and sweet water. Killed three more quail. No deer tracks in the montes along the mesa. A great clamor of geese below us, but we arrived just in time to see seven bunches strung out back

16

for El Doctor. These had been using Widgeon Lake, which is on one of the 'canales' and is salt, not sweet. Evidently then, the geese do not come there for fresh water. Probably they come for gravel, of which there is plenty, though we can recall none below.

Above Widgeon Lake is a big salt lake on which were cormorant, spoonbill, ruddies, avocets, yellowlegs, widgeons, willet, jacksnipe, and two kinds of sandpipers in flocks, one very tiny, the other about the size of a jacksnipe. There were no goose tracks. Also saw coots, grebes, vermilion flycatchers, kingfisher, and black phoebe, and a small white gull with red bill and dark wing tips (royal tern?).

Coming back we sighted a huge 'chimney' of cranes wheeling high in the sky over the Punta. When they got the glint of the sun they showed pure white and looked like a huge sky-rocket bursting into white sparks. Gradually they worked east and when over us suddenly formed into a series of 'V's and started for El Doctor. Carl counted 130 when they were in this

17

formation. They still showed white and looked like great draped strings of pearls against the blue. At no time did they utter a sound. I cannot see how sandhill cranes could show so white. Could they have been whooping cranes?

Killed another quail at camp, and packed up for a before-daylight hike to Widgeon Lake after geese.

2 November, Thursday (Goose Day)

Up at 4 a.m. and hiking across the mesa by 5 a.m. Left our stuff packed with a note for Francisco to haul it back to Coyote Camp. Very interesting making our way in the dark, especially breaking through the cane and cachinilla to the Rillito. Got to the goose bar well before sun-up but nothing there except ducks. About seven Carl started up to Salt Lake to see if the geese were there. He had barely left when a big white flock swung in over the mesa and headed for the blind on set wings. They came over about 30 yards high. If I had shot sideways into the line it would have rained geese, but I didn't want to chase any cripples. So I took the two end ones overhead and killed both stone dead. By now Carl was back and we were starting a war dance when another bunch came in sight. Carl took the gun. They got between him and the sun but he got one dead. Immediately came another bunch, out of which Carl made a pretty double. Then another, and I made a double. This made seven, which was enough. We were hungry, so went up to the lighting place and hid under a tornillo, where we were demolishing cold roast quail and sourdough biscuits when a single came in and lit within what we afterward paced at 18 yards. We suspended lunch and motions, and scarcely breathed for five minutes while we watched him—except Flick, who couldn't make his eyes behave, in spite of my hand on his collar. Finally the single got nervous and left, but along came 11 more and lit within 25 yards. We watched them a long

18

time. These geese keep up a continual hum of small talk not audible at a distance. We plainly saw them go after the coarse sand immediately after setting down. Their wing coverts drape down over their primaries like heron plumes. Some always have their heads up. When they begin shaking their heads they are getting ready to go. At this time they line up in pairs facing the wind, so that they spring up in formation.

The seven we had killed made a he-load packing them down to Coyote Camp. On the way we saw sign, probably coyote but possibly coon, containing a mass of the hard wings of Dytescus beetles, hair, and tornillo beans. At Coyote Camp we had a swim and then Alex Sorteon and Francisco arrived. In the afternoon we ran down to see La Bolsa. The tide was in. It didn't look bad for canoe work. They say sharks come up this far. On the way back we saw four huge black frigate birds flying east. Also saw a peculiar buzzard that must have been a caracara. Goose roasted in the dutch oven tonight. Saw a coyote near camp in the moonlight. Weighed up the geese. They broke the scales but weighed about 5¼ pounds each. One of the brick-tinged young ones was so tender that the skin pulled off with the breast feathers.

3 November, Friday

To El Doctor with Sorteon. Arrived about 10 a.m. There were lots of teal, blue and green-wing, of which Carl killed three. Three geese came over rather high. I shot behind with the first barrel but dropped one dead with the second. The big springs pours up right in the cat-tails—and is warm but fine and sweet. A huge wheeling flock of sandhill cranes passed by going south. After lunch a flock of about 100 geese lit in the lagoon in front of us. Posted Alex for a pass shot while we went around and flushed. He hit two but both got away.

The mirage effects here are remarkable. It looks as if the

19

whole world were a goose swamp, but everything in the way of water over half a mile distant is likely to prove non-existent, as are the beautiful alamos that stand on its shores and the lines of fowl that seem to be setting on its sandbars. Alex says that wells sunk here rise with the tide, and that there is one place where on puncturing the mud with a stick a column of water as high as a man spouts out.

We left rather reluctantly and at dark arrived below San Luis, where Alex dropped us on a fine grassy bank of the Rillito while he went in to bring the canoe down in the morning.

4 November, Saturday

We celebrated washday and shaved off some very long beards. Repacked the outfit for boat work. Alex arrived with the boat about 9 a.m. Stowed cargo and embarked on the Rillito. Found lots of exercise, in the form of two bridges and three beaver dams, two of which we had to portage; also many log jams and fallen trees which we had to cut out. Going over one of the latter we pulled a tenderfoot trick in letting the canoe down on the stub of a limb. This poked a clean hole an inch in diameter right through her bottom, so we had to haul up and become a dry-dock crew. With a piece of tin from a tin can, a piece of canvas, and white lead we contrived a patch that never leaked a drop.

Some interesting scenery, much willow cotton, many herons, but few ducks. At sunset a Cocopa boy riding bareback came out on the bank while we were making another portage around a willow thicket. He swore in English before he saw us but could speak neither English nor Spanish when we asked him how far to the Hidalgo ranch.

Earlier in the afternoon we stepped ashore at an Indian clearing and found some fine melons. At sunset we passed a skunk on the bank. While I cooked supper Carl stepped out

20

and killed a couple of quail and a dove. Night was very cold.

5 November, Sunday

Started about 10 a.m. after letting some clothes dry. Better going today, although we had to portage around one log jam and chop our way through several others and a dozen windfalls. Very pretty traveling along the Rillito, with frequent grassy banks and handsome white-barked cottonwoods. Saw many herons and hawks and horned owls, also many coon and beaver tracks, but no deer. Shortly after lunch we reached the Hidalgo ranch but the old man was not at home. His rather attractive daughter was very polite but could tell us nothing about the country, and her beau, who was on deck in very neat cowpuncher's clothes, could have but didn't. Camped above the ranch and Carl went on a quail hunt. Got two, and half a dozen doves. I fished and caught many small catfish but none big enough to clean. Set a coon trap baited with a live catfish in a wet cowtrack, also quail cleanings; then joined Carl. We saw, or rather heard, an enormous covey in a patch of tall weeds, but they were hard to work and easy to miss.

The doves killed today were full of wild melon seed.

Had a fine supper of teal, dove, quail, mashed potatoes, and C.S.L.-brand sourdough biscuits. A fine camp.

6 November, Monday (C.S.L.)

Ten o'clock saw us headed somewhere southwest—canoe, baggage, and personnel aboard Señor Hidalgo's spring wagon. It was rough, dusty going except along the Rillito, which we soon left, taking a course across a semi-desert, almost treeless, delta plain. Lunched in the edge of a pigweed patch—Aldo got four quail with four shells.

Steady travel all afternoon—we passed Laroma's cow camp

in a beautiful grassy bosque and at 4 p.m. stopped at another camp to ask information. There were hundreds of quail and many doves. We added six quail to our larder. With only a mile to the river, but no road, we decided to try and make it before sundown. It was tough work for the team, through

heavy arrowweed and many small flood-water gullies. But with big bosque ahead and the air full of cormorants and ducks our hopes were high until we encountered a small muddy slough. A sashay on foot showed no way to get ahead; it was almost dark so we camped down in the smoothest available spot. Hidalgo's yarns provided the evening's entertainment.

7 November, Tuesday (C.S.L.)

Quail roosted in the mesquite bush within six feet of our

22

lean-to, flying out as we got up for an early start. Aldo got breakfast while I prospected north along the slough. Located a big lagoon and as I walked back toward camp, surprised a bobcat on the open mud bank. Got in two .30-.30 shots before the cat made cover. Flick trailed a few yards and barked. It took a .32 to finish the job. The cat hung from shoulder to heel. Aldo skinned her out.

We finally got into the river and found it a beautiful large stream—banks overgrown with drooping willows. Considerable beaver and some deer tracks. Made permanent camp about a mile upstream in a mesquite orchard. Quail are everywhere but this is venado country so we are keeping quiet. A paddle up-river before supper netted an appetite. The quail would not be enticed by our candle lantern.

8 November, Wednesday

Made an expedition by canoe, getting off shortly after sun-up. At the point where the lagoon joins the river, we became actors in the famous game of pussy-in-a-corner. Carl, who had the bow, sighted a big bobcat fishing on the small island that forms the point. We promptly got in between the island and shore and had the old bob cornered in a willow thicket. Carl went ashore with the shotgun and stood guard while I backed out the boat to drive her out. It was too easy. She came out between us, hell bent for election. We didn't wake up till she had made a fifteen foot jump across the little channel, when I bid her Godspeed with an ineffectual shot into the jungle. It was inconceivable that this cat could get away from us. But she did.

On down the river (*what* river Lord only knows—it may be the Santa Clara, the Pescadero, or the Bee) Carl sighted another cat in a willow thicket. He made a quick shot and knocked her down but she got up and kept going. We went ashore and tried to trail her but no luck.

23

About two miles below camp the river began to break up and we soon encountered a complete log jam which stopped all further progress. I used to talk pretty bravely about wiggling through the Labyrinth of the Colorado, of which this is probably the head. But we learned something on the Rillito. Neither of us had any desire to travel through that log jam.

Coming back we caught a wet cormorant by diving him down. He put up quite a fight with his hooked bill. Set him out for live bait at one of the cat sets. Also set two beaver traps.

In the evening we explored upstream, finding great fields of hemp and arrowweed but few deer tracks. Built a quail trap out of dead arrowweed as we needed meat and did not want to shoot around camp.

Every evening a great flight of cormorants comes into the lagoon from the north, and every morning they go out. Around camp, in camp, and in fact all over are incredible numbers of quail. Also many doves. A few ducks fly over the lagoon.

This night a beaver kept slapping the river right by camp. Sounded like a large heavy boulder plumping into the water. We have a grass bed and sleep with great comfort.

9 November, Thursday

Up before sun and eastward up the lagoon. Great droves of herons and cormorants accumulated before us like a round-up. Much fine mesquite and grass country on the banks, and very little current. About four or five miles up we found many fine big mallards. Lagoon broken up into several live and several dead channels, the former very swift and navigable only with difficulty. Found very few deer tracks.

After lunch and a nap we decided to lay in some meat, so I killed a greenhead and Carl got 13 quail. We found that in walking through the wild hemp one can gather quite a lot of beans by simply holding the hands cupped and letting the beans rain in from overhead. Killed a couple of coots for trap bait. Killed a duckhawk chasing a heron.

On the way back we were suddenly aware that a great caterwauling going on in the jungle to our left was not the usual croaking and fighting of herons and fowl, but rather a real, genuine, back-alley cat fight, with claws, whiskers, and all the trimmings. We quickly headed for the racket but the wind was dead against us, and when the fight got fairly in our lee it suddenly ceased. We caught a glimpse of one of the parties to the controversy sneaking off under the shadows, but not enough to shoot at.

Our live bait had got loose. We shall henceforth trail a piéce of blue bacon strung over the boundless green miles of the Delta. We rebaited with coot. Saw an egret just below camp; also a few white herons and many buzzards. Carl took a still hunt on the point before supper and found much fresh deer sign.

10 November, Friday

Organized a deer drive. I sat in the lane near camp while Carl still-hunted the east side of the point. Then he sat while I hunted out the west side. This took till noon but no deer, although they made fresh tracks within 20 yards of camp last night. At the point I found a Mexican black hawk in one of the traps we had baited with a coot. Hawks and buzzards are so plentiful that one cannot leave any bait exposed.

Carl caught a large mullet on his throw line this noon.

We each saw a cat this morning, but neither shot for fear of spoiling the deer hunt. Carl had a dead-sure chance at his. One can often locate cats by listening to the scolding of the quail, which are so nearly ubiquitous that one can follow anybody or anything through the woods by the quail scolding and flushing.

25

We took an evening hunt below Campo del Gato. Found numerous tracks in a big mesquite park. Carl missed a coyote which almost ran into him. The cormorants were roosting in the willows as we came home.

11 November, Saturday

We paddled up the river all morning against a strong current. Found an old corral and killed a mess of quail after lunch. Saw another flock of cranes wheeling eastward over the lagoon.

The river becomes swift and narrow about two miles above camp, and is lined with down willows.

Hunted the point again this evening. Carl found a hard mud slough on which he thought fawns had been playing since our last hunt yesterday morning. I stood at a pass and tried to count the cormorant flocks coming in, but gave it up. There must be several thousand. They roost in the trees, but unless their perch is very high above the water they hit the water first in order to get the benefit of their feet in taking flight. When they are disturbed at night it is doubtful if they can again take to trees. If not they may spend the night on the water, and this may account for the few flightless individuals one always finds on the lagoon and on the river.

We reset one of the traps for cat just above camp, baiting with the remains of the mallard and quail.

12 November, Sunday

First made the rounds of the traps, which we had not visited yesterday. The beaver trap was sprung but empty. We reset it in a different place. The bobcat trap contained a small coon. He looked very wet and lonesome, but his hide looked fair so we skinned him out and reset. He had been in a day and the glands under the pit of his caught foreleg had become swollen and inflamed. Cased his hide and made another deer hunt of the Del Gato mesquite orchard. The wind changed on us and furthermore we had moved from mesquite country into hemp. We saw ravens sitting near where Carl hit the coyote on 10 November. I have no doubt he is about there, dead, but we couldn't find him.

Coming back we saw seven mallards light in the little channel where Carl killed his cat. Made a sneak and I missed a big greenhead with both barrels, but I got a hen with a third shell. She flushed late and tried to follow the others. Flick retrieved her promptly from the arrowweed.

Carl saw the cranes again this morning—a huge flock. He says they are white with black wing tips.

Paddling home we again heard a loud splashing under a patch of cane near the creek. I'm pretty sure it is a beaver who airs and suns himself there. Or maybe a coon.

27

In evening went north on the east bank and killed 14 quail for carne seco. Smoked them over mesquite coals that evening. Quite a little deer sign up there. Quail, noodles, and cornbread for supper, with raisin preserves. A big mesquite fire to celebrate our last evening in camp, and made plans for one last try at the deer.

13 November, Monday

Up extra early and started up the lagoon, after looking at our traps, one of which contained a dead buzzard. A fine bunch of mallards on the lagoon but we didn't dare shoot. A little above the old corral Carl sighted a whole bunch of animals on shore under a patch of cane and mesquite. We hoped they were cats but as we stole up in the canoe we saw they were a whole family of coons. I took the shotgun and killed one dead with the first barrel and thought I'd killed the big one with the second. The big one disappeared, however, so we put Flick on his trail and he soon barked about a hundred yards up the bank in a dense mesquite thicket full of deep mud. We rushed up and found the big crippled one under a pile of dead brush. These coons were big and fat and in better fur than the previous one.

Went on up the lagoon and made a hunt on the north bank but found very few tracks. As usual, great numbers of quail and doves. Then while eating some lunch we drifted down the lagoon and went ashore on the point to skin out coons and incidentally to watch for mallards, which had been passing regularly. They continued to pass, but always saw us and the snow-white coons, which were so covered with fat as to look like big lumps of lard. The young one skinned out a lot easier than the old one.

Back to camp, regretfully taking up the traps as we went. Carl had another mullet on his throw line. Lost his pipe in the lagoon shooting at some teal. Packed up the outfit, including the grass bed, and took our final paddle down the river to the Campo del Gato, where we were just setting up for the night when Hidalgo arrived with his team, as per appointment. Roast mallard dinner to celebrate our last night in camp. At evening heard a whistling in the swamp which Hidalgo said was a beaver. At bedtime heard geese passing downstream from us, going east. These were the only geese we saw or heard in this region.

14 November, Tuesday

Up extra early and breakfast over by sun-up. Did not replenish the sourdough—the empty kettle a sad symbol of bright days gone by. Hit the Cachorrilla while the morning sun sculptured old Sierra Mayor into changing shapes and shadows. Fine fresh breeze from the north.

In the calabasas fields myriad quail were out feeding and whistling in welcome of the warm sunlight. Walked along beside the wagon and killed a last fine mess of 14 birds.

White herons sat on the lagoons to the north as we passed. Saw five pelicans passing as we crossed the big chamise flats. Killed a sharpshin. Reached Hidalgo's by noon and were his guests for luncheon. The wind blew gusts of sand through the wattle walls of his dining hall as we ate tamales and drank coffee. The pet pig, Flick, two dogs, five children, and a black mare stood guard by the door, watchful for the crumbs of the master's table, and sortied into the hall when the crumbs failed to materialize. A little white-toothed, dusky-faced boy haunted Flick's side trying to feed him watermelon, and repeating over and over again some kind of assurance that sandias were fine food for dogs. A sick little girl, wrapped in a shabby overcoat, sat in a dim corner and watched us with great soft eyes. And all the while our host poured coffee and recounted with gusto

29

and large gestures brave tales of the days when he was a free-lance vaquero seeking fortune and adventure on the Arizona frontier. Of adventure he found great store—of fortune, many a fair beginning. Meanwhile the wind blew gusts of sand, the little boy chanted to Flick of watermelons, and the little girl looked with great eyes upon us. Finally the coffee pot went dry, and we started.

Arrived at San Luis before sundown, and hopped a ride on a load of beef hides into Yuma, where we arrived about 8 p.m. A bath, a call on our good friend Colonel Fly, and we caught a midnight train for home.

Country

There is much confusion between land and country. Land is the place where corn, gullies, and mortgages grow. Country is the personality of land, the collective harmony of its soil, life, and weather. Country knows no mortgages, no alphabetical agencies, no tobacco road; it is calmly aloof to these petty exigencies of its alleged owners. That the previous occupant of my farm was a bootlegger mattered not one whit to its grouse; they sailed as proudly over the thickets as if they were guests of a king.

Poor land may be rich country, and vice versa. Only economists mistake physical opulence for riches. Country may be rich despite a conspicuous poverty of physical endowment, and its quality may not be apparent at first glance, nor at all times.

I know, for example, a certain lakeshore, a cool austerity of pines and wave-washed sands. All day you see it only as something for the surf to pound, a dark ribbon that stretches farther than you can paddle, a monotony to mark the miles by. But toward sunset some vagrant breeze may waft a gull across a headland, behind which a sudden roistering of loons reveals the presence of a hidden bay. You are seized with an impulse to land, to set foot on bearberry carpets, to pluck a balsam

31

bed, to pilfer beach plums or blueberries, or perhaps to poach a partridge from out those bosky quietudes that lie behind the dunes. A bay? Why not also a trout stream? Incisively the paddles clip little soughing swirls athwart the gunwale, the bow swings sharp shoreward and cleaves the greening depths for camp.

Later, a supper-smoke hangs lazily upon the bay; a fire flickers under drooping boughs. It is a lean poor land, but rich country.

Some woods, perennially lush, are notably lacking in charm. Tall clean-boled oaks and tulip poplars may be good to look at, from the road, but once inside one may find a coarseness of minor vegetation, a turbidity of waters, and a paucity of wild-life. I cannot explain why a red rivulet is not a brook. Neither can I, by logical deduction, prove that a thicket without the potential roar of a quail covey is only a thorny place. Yet every outdoorsman knows that this is true. That wildlife is merely something to shoot at or to look at is the grossest of fallacies. It often represents the difference between rich country and mere land.

There are woods that are plain to look at, but not to look into. Nothing is plainer than a cornbelt woodlot; yet, if it be August, a crushed pennyroyal, or an over-ripe mayapple, tells you here is a place. October sun on a hickory nut is irrefutable evidence of good country; one senses not only hickory but a whole chain of further sequences: perhaps of oak coals in the dusk, a young squirrel browning, and a distant barred owl hilarious over his own joke.

The taste for country displays the same diversity in aesthetic competence among individuals as the taste for opera, or oils. There are those who are willing to be herded in droves through 'scenic' places; who find mountains grand if they be proper mountains, with waterfalls, cliffs, and lakes. To such the Kansas plains are tedious. They see the endless corn, but not the heave and the grunt of ox teams breaking the prairie. History, for them, grows on campuses. They look at the low hori-

zon, but they cannot see it, as de Vaca did, under the bellies of the buffalo.

In country, as in people, a plain exterior often conceals hidden riches, to perceive which requires much living in and with. Nothing is more monotonous than the juniper foothills, until some veteran of a thousand summers, laden blue with berries, explodes in a blue burst of chattering jays. The drab sogginess of a March cornfield, saluted by one honker from the sky, is drab no more.

Canada, 1924

A.L., C.S.L., F.L., A.S.L.

P. O. Ely, Minn.

11 June, 1924

'Twas Wednesday noon when we set sail from Winton, Minnesota, going up Fall Lake in an old launch, thence by truck over an old logging grade four miles into the SW arm of Basswood Lake. Here we loaded up our two 16-foot Racine canoes and struck NE for the international boundary. About 5:00 p.m. we got to the Canadian Ranger Station (Quetico Provincial Park), bought our licenses from Ranger Seeley, headed north about a mile, and pitched camp. Starker's fishing fever was running high, so we paddled out to a little island and caught two pickerel for supper.

Our camp was under a fine stand of Norway pine, where hermit thrushes were singing. It is already apparent that the pine timber on the Canadian side is all uncut and not much burned, while on the American side there is not a pine left. Fortunately the numerous islands are all covered with fine mature pines.

Roast pickerel for supper. When we went to bed at nine it wasn't yet dark.

12 June

About 4:30 a.m. gave up trying to stay in bed. While eating breakfast saw a black mallard and several small mergansers pass by. Headed north toward Canadian Point, where **in a**

wide part of the lake we found a big bunch of loons, the **banks** of pine timber echoing their calls. Starker trolled and caught **a** big pickerel with a parasitic worm projecting from his side. In spite of this he was fat. Put him back, of course. About 10 a.m. reached the Basswood River and soon got to the first falls, portaging around them and finding our outfit good to carry but not quite to the point where we could make it in one trip. Had some lunch, and Carl and Fritz caught two fine wall-eyed pike, in addition to pickerel which we let go. Several red-breasted mergansers passed over. Then we portaged the lower falls, at the foot of which Fritz added another wall-eye and Starker caught a pickerel. About 3 p.m. we camped on the portage of still another very pretty waterfall which is probably the end of the river and the beginning of Crooked Lake. There is considerable style to this camp, which is on a grassy knoll overlooking the falls, with an International Boundary Monument for a tent peg.

Boiled wall-eyed pike with mustard sauce for supper. After supper we fed an Indian who chanced along in a birchbark canoe, and then went fishing. Carl flirted with a huge pike at the foot of the falls, but couldn't hook him. Fritz caught another wall-eye but put him back. After threatening rain it cleared up with a beautiful sunset. Fished again—Starker caught a wall-eye all on his own—he is learning to throw a spoon—and Carl caught the granddaddy of the white-eyed tribe, a beautiful big four-pounder. This was on one of the jointed plugs. Everybody caught pike. Turned in at 9:00 after 17½ hours. Even then it wasn't fully dark.

13 June

Got under way about 7:00. Rounding a point near the painted cliffs Fritz and Starker saw two does. Carl and I came up and tried to photograph one of them which broke and ran at 40 yards. The scenery is extraordinary. Went up a blind bay by mistake and found a muskeg with moose tracks. They had evidently come down for the lily which has a rosette of red leaves on the bottom. Moose tracks were visible in the lake bottom as well as on the shore.

36

Soon we came to a narrows with a current literally full of big pike—we caught several and let them go.

No sooner had we started on than I sighted two deer on a grassy shore. Carl and I made the sneak. They seemed to see us at a quarter mile but resumed feeding and playing like a pair of puppies, striking with their front feet and dodging sideways. They, too, were after the red lilies, fragments of which were floating in the water. We had both the wind and the light in our favor and got up to not more than 30 yards, snapping two films.

We nooned on a fine point of solid rock, open to the breeze, with deep pitchoffs full of big pike, and big shiners along the shoreline. Fritz caught a 7¾ pounder, and Starker a smaller one and a wall-eye. Many grouse were drumming here. A pair of tree swallows had a nest in a woodpecker hole in an old jack pine. The hole was alive with big red ants. How the young would survive the ants I can't imagine.

Continuing through Crooked Lake I caught a big wall-eye of 5¼ pounds, which we kept for supper. Camped on a little rock island with only half a dozen trees and no mosquitoes. Tried a fish mulligan consisting of the planked wall-eye cut into big boneless cubes, ham, potatoes, mixed dehydrated vegetables, rice, and noodles. It was a huge success. We had the broth first (thus avoiding any need for a hot drink) and the rest afterward. It was so good we christened it 'Island Mulligan,' and the camp, 'Mulligan Island.'

After supper Fritz and Starker went back to a narrows with a strong current where we had seen many wall-eyes, while Carl and I went trolling for trout. We were soon diverted, however, by a persistent bawling across the lake, which we took to be either a bear cub (which bawls very much like a calf) or a calf moose. We landed and found a lake with a little muskeg full of moose tracks, beds, trails, and piles of sign. By this time the bawling had stopped, as the wind was quartering against us. We lifted the canoe over and found we were on an arm connecting with the channel where the boys were fishing. They had landed a huge pike and were playing another one at a place where the pike had run a school of shiners up into the shore rocks and had them surrounded. The minnows were dashing frantically while the pike slashed right and left in the shallows. One could hook a pike at nearly every cast. Fritz had de-barbed a spoon in order to facilitate getting them off for release. Everybody caught pike (and a few wall-eyes) till the mosquitoes and approaching dark sent us to camp, towing the two big ones to have their pictures taken tomorrow.

We distinctly heard grouse drumming at 9:30 p.m. after dark. The moon was nearly full. Hermit thrushes were also singing.

14 June

Up a little later this morning and got started about 7:00. Trolled for trout a while but caught nothing but small pickerel. Continued west through the channels of Crooked Lake. A party of Indians, headed for La Croix, passed us. Arrived at Curtain Falls for lunch. Two miles before we got there we could hear the roar, and a quarter mile away one could feel the moist cool air full of spray vapor. The falls are really quite a show.

A pileated woodpecker flew across the channel near the falls. We had heard them previously drumming in the woods.

At the falls we had a pow-wow and decided to strike off north into the wilder country rather than continue along the Indian route near Shortess Island. We went down the first bay, where we mistakenly supposed the portage to be, and discovered a little hidden lake on which was an eagle. Moose, deer,

38

and bear tracks, all fresh, were seen on the sand beach at its outlet.

On a bare rock in this bay we found a nest of three young herring gulls. The old ones flew overhead and tried to lead us away. The young took to the water as we approached. We ran one down and caught it—a pretty downy chick, white with black dots. It did not dive, but swam well; however, the down plumage soaked up water rather rapidly.

We now tried the second bay and found the portage. A big buck, whose fresh tracks we found in the sand, snorted and stampeded up the hill as we landed. Saw two grouse and the tracks of both moose and deer on the portage. Crossed an unnamed lake and then portaged into Roland Lake. It was immediately apparent that we had here the green water of the real north country, rather than the brown water of Crooked and Basswood Lakes. We camped on a beautiful rock point full of reindeer moss and backed by pines. Hermit thrushes serenaded us at supper, and a loon called from a far bay. Starker, as usual, started to fish, and from the canoe landing hooked what we supposed (from his spots) to be a small pickerel, but he fought as no pickerel ever did. On landing him we found him to be a beautifully spotted lake trout. This was on a barbless spoon—which we shall use hereafter. Starker got two more trout. We have had two big ambitions—seeing moose and catching trout, and have now solved the trout problem.

After supper Fritz stumbled upon a hen mallard setting eight eggs right in the pine forest. The number of adventures awaiting us in this blessed country seems without end. Watching the gray twilight settling upon our lake we could truly say that 'all our ways are pleasantness and all our paths are peace.'

15 June

Fried lake trout for breakfast were positively the sweetest fish ever eaten.

All the trout on stringers were dead. Have never yet found a way to keep trout alive, short of a tight pen in the water.

A fine chorus of white-throated sparrows when the sun came up. Their note sounds like 'Ah, poor Canada!' Thank the Lord for country as poor as this.

We had a laundering and sewing bee around camp. Then explored the lake and found tomorrow's portage into Trout Lake. Trolled to the sand beach, where we found fresh moose tracks and had a fine but brief swim, the water being cold. Coming back to camp we photographed the mallard nest. The nest consisted of a hollow pushed into the dry litter under the overhanging branches of a little spruce. It had a perfect circle of a rim consisting of the gray down of the hen. The behavior of the hen was entirely different when approached from the water instead of the land—from the land she played cripple, whereas from the water she sprang directly into the air and hardly quacked. Only eight eggs and nest full.

While we were boiling tea for lunch, Starker caught another trout. After a nap all round we engaged in the very serious occupation of catching perch minnows to be used as bait for the evening fishing. Later I made Starker a bow of white cedar. In the evening we caught a few trout, one of which we had for supper. It was a female and had pink flesh, whereas the previous ones had white flesh. Only small fish were caught on first casts, indicating that big ones get used to a spoon and no longer get excited about it. The first three minnows also drew bites, but later minnows wouldn't work.

Carl and I learned something while casting in a bay behind camp. The water was covered with willow cotton, which gummed up the line and the ferrules so as to make casting nearly impossible.

At dark a solitary loon serenaded us with his lonesome call, which Fritz imitates very well. This call seems to prevail at night, while the laughing call is used during the day. Carl remembers the laughing call at night, however, on the trip we made to Drummond Island with Dad about 1905.

The Lord did well when he put the loon and his music into this lonesome land.

16 June

Under way by 7:00 and over the portage into Trout Lake. A stiff SW wind gave us a little tussle getting across into the islands. From here we skirted the lee shores on an exploration trip into the SW arm, where in a fine sand-beach bay we noticed all the cedars were defoliated up to a six-foot 'high-water mark.' We landed to investigate and decided it was undoubtedly a winter 'deer yard,' the occasional spruces not being trimmed up. The cedars overhanging the water along the shoreline had undoubtedly been browsed-off from the ice.

We rigged a couple of shirt-tail sails, put the canoes side by side, and returned up the lake 'four sheets to the wind,' trolling as we went. We hooked a big fish which proved to be a four-pound trout. He was hooked severely, so we kept him for supper. We then attached the little barbless spoon and at once hooked a small trout, indicating that the size of the lure has a good deal to do with the size of the fish.

Lunched on a little dream of an island consisting of a single tree on a single rock. Looked like rain, so we decided not to push on to Darkey Lake. Got up the tent and hustled in some wood from across the channel just in time before she came down in sheets, whereupon we holed up and made some stew.

41

RAINY DAY OBSERVATIONS

Carl: The nice thing about this country is that there is no cut lumber on the shorelines. We haven't seen a sawed board since we left Basswood Lake.

Fritz: We don't know where we're going but we always get there. Following lakeshore on the big lakes there is seldom more than one way to go and a man always knows what's at the end of it. Up here there are twenty ways and every one different.

Starker: There are no Indians or tourists to bother us. We've seen one last-year's camp since we left Curtain Falls.

A new leech—first seen in Roland Lake. Olive green with orange lines on each side and a row of orange dots along the dorsal line.

Lichens—our rock island is covered with gray lichens, which in dry weather flatten out and expose only their 'rubberized' upper surfaces, thus allowing a minimum of evaporation. The minute a drop of water strikes them, this surface turns olive green and the outer edges curl up, exposing the rough absorptive under-surface to the rain. The individual plants must attain great age, since we have passed numerous places where initials have persisted for years by being scraped into the lichen covers of rocks.

Toward evening it cleared beautifully and we all went fishing. Caught several small ones and then came back for supper (trout chowder and very good). After supper about sundown we noticed trout wallowing on the surface and gave them a try. Fritz hooked a whale, which we played hard for 36 minutes. The fish sounded with extreme persistence. Finally Fritz brought him in and the barbless spoon fell out of his mouth as he hit the bottom of the boat. He weighed six pounds and was 28¾″ long. Tied him up over night and next morning took his picture before letting him go. He was a wonderful fish and one of the hardest fighters imaginable. The loons called and whitethroats sang as we were playing him, and before we had him home the full moon hung in the east and we had to read the scales by the firelight.

17 June

Packed up and under way by a little after seven. It was a clear sparkling day with a stiff north breeze. We found the portage into Darkey Lake very steep and full of fallen fire-killed pine. On the second trip we bumped right into a pair of partridges with at least ten or a dozen chicks, of which we caught two to take a photo. The old hen had a number of calls, one a hiss like a bull snake, to defy the enemy; another a cluck like a hen to reassure the brood to sit tight; another a meow like a catbird, evidently meaning alarm; also an alarm chirp like a Gambel quail. I'm not sure the hen gave all these calls—both she and the cock were on deck all the time, trying to save the day. The chicks had a peep just like any chick. They were in the down—I should guess less than a week old.

Looked for the Indian paintings supposed to be found on the cliffs in the lower part of Darkey Lake but couldn't find them. The water we find is intermediate—not so green as Trout Lake and not so brown as Crooked Lake. It has an outlet, and we found later that it contains pike, perch, wall-eyes, trout, and, unfortunately, carp.

Explored the northwest arm down to the outlet, hoping to find bass. We are sure we saw some small ones. At the outlet we found big three- and four-pound carp in great numbers. Had a lot of fun gigging or snagging them with a spoon. I also tried a bow and arrow and later a spear with a nail lashed to the point. The spear worked right now—with the very first shot I got a big one right through the back. These carp were active, hard, and nicely colored, and were spawning. When the spawn dropped from hooked fish, great numbers of minnows gathered to eat it.

Coming back up the arm Fritz and I saw a doe and snapped her, and I caught a huge pike with the tail of a one-pound fish projecting from his throat. We had hooked no bass, so we all set out to catch some supper, using the fine minnows Starker had caught at the outlet. Rigged a bobber and fished off our rock point by camp, where I caught a big trout for supper. After supper we caught a big pike and some wall-eyes, all of which we turned back.

18 June

We were all lazy this morning and slept until about 6:30. The last hour in bed was spent slaughtering large blood-filled mosquitoes that in one way or another had found their way under our netting. Our camp on Darkey was a beautiful one on a high promontory with exceptionally deep water on three sides. Left camp about 8:00 with a strong head wind from the east. The first of five portages to Bunt Lake turned out to be a lining proposition but the other four were bona fide portages—the roughest we have struck to date.

Launched our canoes in a rough bit of water and paddled out to a small Norway-pine island where we had lunch.

After lunch we continued on east to the northeast end of the channel connecting the main east and west sections of the lake; a particularly attractive spot because there is less evidence of fire than in any of the country we have struck so far.

Made camp on the westernmost of a string of four small islands. Camp is made up in apple-pie order because we expect to spend two days here.

In the way of miscellaneous information, the deer we saw

yesterday was feeding on young horse-tail just coming up out of the water.

Found beaver lodges both in dead water in narrow inland channels and on the open lakeshore with a mile or more of open water offshore.

In exploring the details of our island I heard a continued peep-peeping and on investigating found a laughing loon's nest containing one chick and one partly hatched egg with a live chick peeping inside. The egg is very large—about the size of a goose egg; color a dull brown with a few black flecks scattered irregularly. The chick is slate gray in color with black feet and bill and whitish belly.

During supper the old loons watched us from a distance of sixty yards. But after supper when we all disappeared into the tent where we kept very quiet, the hen loon took courage and came right up to within thirty feet of our white tent and just now she has the chick out in the water with her. The rooster is off about forty yards making reassuring small talk to the hen while she takes the chances.

19 June (C.S.L.)

Heavy rain from about 4:00 until 7:00—we were busy dodging leaks in the tent. After a good rainy-weather breakfast Aldo set the pace by shaving and washing clothes—Fritz, Starker, and I soon followed suit and the camp was and still is bedraped with garments of many shapes. Weather too uncertain for travel so we spent the forenoon fixing up generally; baked a big batch of tortillas.

Our loon was on the nest and remained there all morning. Her mate dove into the nest evidently bringing food. The nest is just 25 feet from our tent.

An early lunch was ready when we discovered a young bull moose swimming the channel to the west of our camp. We launched a canoe and raced the moose back to the south shore, coming within six feet of his posterior as he heaved himself out of the water into the spruce thicket. Aldo took two pictures.

While we ate lunch a beautiful white-tail doe browsed along shore just east of camp. She was quite reddish.

In the afternoon we explored an uncharted bay south of camp. Aldo caught a pike and two wall-eyes for our supper. Fritz baked a whacking corn bread, and noodles completed the menu.

The loon story is closed. The second chick evidently hatched this morning and the parents proceeded to move their chicks to a safer place. The older chick made off at the parents call but the weaker one was left behind. Fritz and I have just taken it up to another island some distance from camp in hopes that the old loons will find it.

20 June

Up bright and early, packed up, and under way about 6:30. Eastward along Brent Lake, which has much spruce shore and many high bold islands. Saw a blue-wing teal and another pair of loons with two tiny chicks trailing them. Down the SE arm of Brent and over a beautiful portage into a little unnamed lake, where we bumped into another pair of loons, one with the young on her back. Another portage put us into McIntyre Lake. We got as far as the narrows when the heavy sea in the SW arm led us to try to portage out of the SE arm, which was calm. We found an old trail about half a mile long into Sarah Lake. On the trail we found some lovely pink lady's-slipper in a swamp, and a mother partridge with a bunch of chicks even smaller than the ones we saw a few days ago. The old hen whined exactly like a puppy dog when we approached the chicks, and played the cripple act to perfection when we started away. She kept ahead of us, leading us almost to the lake.

This portage is through beautiful birch timber with an undergrowth of maple brush and hazel. It has never been cleared but has been used at odd times. On it we found some wolf or bear sign with a big gathering of tiger-swallowtail butterflies on it.

Before leaving McIntyre we saw a big, light-red deer on a rocky point. The water in McIntyre was very high. Could raise no fish.

Cooked lunch near a beaver lodge in the foot of the NE arm of Sarah Lake. More fresh cuttings on the shores (mostly aspen and alder) than any place we have yet seen. In several places recently we have seen old dead pine logs gnawed by beaver—evidently just to exercise their teeth.

All of these waters are now covered with a film of jack-pine pollen, which also makes a line on all the rocks in protected places. It does not seem to gum a fishline as the willow cotton does.

Went south on Sarah to just above the narrows, where we made camp on a fine pine island with bold shores and little underbrush. We thought we had got away from our nursery duties but soon found we had camped in a regular kindergarten. Carl found a loon's nest with one hatched egg and a pipped one, while Starker found a nest full of little juncos right where we were pitching our tent. We moved into another place, but the young were soon hopping all through the camp, while the old birds scolded us constantly and our new hen loon complained in the channel behind us.

Tried the fish but there was an east wind and we couldn't connect with anything but a few wall-eyes, which we had for supper.

During the evening we heard a tree crash across the channel—doubtless the work of beavers. Very few mosquitoes during the night so we all slept fine.

21 June

While we were breakfasting three beautiful loons swam up to within 60 yards several times to look us over. Their motive

was evidently curiosity. We have noticed that the trill of the laughing call is produced by vibrating the lower mandible, and not by a mechanism of the throat alone. Also that the 'laugh' seems to prevail as a note of alarm or fear, the lonesome call seldom being used when the loon is worried or alarmed.

Packed a lunch and started out on the trail of the big bass. Tried a little bottlenecked bay just across from camp but could raise nothing on spoons. Then tried the pike-minnow plug and got results forthwith, removing two gangs of hooks to give the fish a chance. Also caught them on a pork-rind spinner. Those caught on a single hook jumped as many as four times; those on a plug never more than once. No plugs for us if we can help it. Carl also caught two huge pike, one on a barbless spoon and the other on a pork rind. Each took forty minutes to land —they were so heavy that the light rod acted exactly as if it were trying to lift a railroad tie. Both pike had scars, and the smaller one a healed nick in his back. Both were the same length but the first one was deeper and heavier. It is impossible to squeeze in the gill covers on these huge fish—they can be lifted only by getting the fingers behind the gills. Even then one's hand would not reach around a much bigger one. Weighed them by using Starker's bow on a paddle, giving the scales three times the leverage of the fish, and multiplying the scale reading by three. Thus we stayed within the capacity of the scales.

We named this Battleship Bay after the huge proportions of the big pike. In it was a large beaver lodge recently extended many feet into the lake by adding sticks of peeled aspen and alder and unpeeled birch. Evidently the birch is not eaten but just cut as building material. The older section of the lodge on the shore end was plastered with gravel and mud—this was evidently the part used last winter.

Broke my glasses while shaving—luckily had an extra pair.

After a fine nap we all went in for a swim, diving off a steep, smooth rock into the deep water. It didn't seem nearly so cold after we got in. Then had a big dinner of bean soup, bass, and tortillas. After supper went back to our bay after bass. They weren't biting, but the beaver show was better. A beaver played around in the mirror-like reflections of the bay, 'pomping' down with a huge splash of water only thirty yards from us. Caught a few wall-eyes and returned to camp.

The narrows at the mouth of the bay are full of deer tracks, plainly visible under four feet of water.

Before we went to bed Fritz several times started all the loons within several miles by giving the 'lonesome' call through his fingers. Some of those that answered him were on McIntyre Lake, way over the hills.

Several times today we thought we could hear a waterfall in the NE arm of Sarah. Tomorrow we are going down there to investigate.

22 June

Off for the NE arm to see what we can see. As we were going down the big channel Starker caught a fine lake trout trolling with the rod. We kept him for supper, as we have unanimously concluded they are way ahead of any other fish.

We soon found our waterfall, which is of brown-stained water, coloring the whole extreme end of the bay. Followed it up and found a little lake, only a hundred yards in from Sarah but 25 feet higher, with its mouth dammed by beaver so that all the shores were flooded. Signs of an old portage to this lake. No suckers in the stream—we looked for some for Starker to shoot with his bow and arrow.

Found no bass in this bay as the water is full of jack-pine pollen, which killed our trout, evidently clogging his gills. There is another but older beaver lodge in this bay.

Caught a few bass but they soon stopped biting, so we decided to climb the high hill to the east and eat lunch there. The view was very interesting—also the vegetation and glaciated dome-like granite. Pink lady's-slipper was common all over the mountain.

It was a bit warm so we all decided to go swimming. We had a fine swim, and seeing a big shoal of minnows we rigged up a dishrag on two sticks and caught a bucketful. This suggested a perch-fishing party, which we tried, but without success. There are no long weeds in any of these lakes and if there are any big perch we haven't seen them.

Now gave the bass a whirl with the minnows. On the way to the bay Fritz and Starker heard a big animal crash into the brush—may have been a moose. Carl and I caught mostly wall-eyes but Fritz and Starker sighted their bass and dangled minnows in front of them and were very successful. Turned them all back. While we were fooling with these bass, a deer snorted at us from the birch woods. It now threatened rain so we scooted for camp and cooked up a fine dinner. Had the dishes washed before the rain hit us, after which we holed up in the tent and played the mouth organ and sang and smoked while the rain beat down and added cheer to the evening. It cleared up and started blowing just before dark, with a fine pale sunset behind the blue clouds. Fritz raised some more loon music by calling them.

23 June

Got under way about 8:00 after taking a picture of Starker's big bass and turning him loose. Had the wind behind us, so hoisted our shirt-tail sails and kited down Sarah in a hurry. Starker caught a fine trout trolling and we kept him for dinner. Tried the bass but couldn't raise any. Over a very steep portage into a little lake full of fresh beaver workings. Tried the bass here and saw many little ones but none big enough to strike. Then into another little lake with much fresh beaver work and several lodges, and a fine little lily-padded bay in one end, with muskeg shores. This lake was remarkably deep with a mud bottom and deep, clear, blue water. Raised no fish. Then over

51

a very short portage into a lake so flooded by old beaver work that all the shore timber was killed. We were so hungry that we ate lunch on a shelving rock. There were many old lodges in this lake but no recent signs of beaver and all the aspen within reach of shore had been cut. It was evidently abandoned. Fritz saw a snowshoe rabbit come down to the lakeshore for a drink. Raised no fish here.

P.S. Mistaken about the fish. After lunch Starker saw a trout pass our point and I soon caught a beauty on a small spoon with a piece of skin off the trout caught in Sarah. This fish had only the faintest suggestion of spots and was of a beautiful brown mottled color. We kept him for supper. Now set about to find our portage but couldn't locate it. Spent the whole afternoon cruising around, locating two lakes to the west and one to the south, which we finally concluded was our lake. Meanwhile we had made camp as it was too late to go on. It proved to be one of our prettiest and most interesting camps. A bunch of loons kept inspecting us and providing the music for the evening. After supper I caught another of the beautiful mottled trout. The feeling of not knowing quite where we were, also a fine bunch of rootless alder wood, made this an exceptionally nice camp.

24 June

Under way about 7 o'clock after an extra-fine breakfast of fried trout, applesauce, and cornbread. Decided to chance it down the beaver dam and soon identified the next lake (Brown Lake) as the one we were looking for. Fredrico Lake, with the beaver dam and duck pond, runs into it from the west. Portaged on into what we called Blue Lake, from the blue water. Fished here and Starker had a strike that seemed to be trout but he caught none. Thence over the forked portage into what we thought was the Ranger Station bay but where we soon found we had another long portage to make. Ate lunch here and called it Basswood Jr., from the brown water.

The forked portage was a long one and we rested halfway. There were very big moose tracks on it. The Blue Lake end has been flooded by beaver and we sank up to our knees in places. We observed that a boggy portage was not necessarily a soft one.

At Basswood Jr. we entered the big burn that devastated the 'civilized' end of our route about 15 years ago. There is an osprey nest on this lake, and old beaver lodges on its shores.

At lunch today Carl looked wise and trotted out three tailor-made cigarettes, which he, with great forbearance, had been carrying in his pocket these two weeks.

We had a fair breeze quartering against us all afternoon, except for a two-mile stretch at the mouth of Pipestem Bay, which we sailed in no time at all. Going up Pipestem we saw a porcupine drinking. After a long drag got over the lower portage just before sunset. Here we saw several canoes—the first human beings we had seen since 14 June, ten days ago. Noticed basswood growing near the falls—evidently it goes this far north only near water that is open the year long and hence modifies the temperature sufficiently to enable the basswood to survive.

Camped on a pretty little island within sound of the falls. We were lucky to have such a nice place for our last camp. Had been paddling and portaging 16 hours so we cooked a big dinner and turned in early.

25 June

Up at 4:30 and found a big loon inspecting our camp. Also saw a black mallard and what seemed to be a bluebill. This country has more marshy bays than do the rock-bound shores where we have been and hence is better adapted to nesting ducks. After a fine breakfast of bacon and fried noodles we sorted our duffel and started out. Soon reached our last portage, where Fritz remarked that there was sign not only of moose but also of elk and knights of Columbus. Even so, we saw a deer in it, in spite of the landing docks, tin cans, and old papers.

Now had a long pull up Fall Lake in the teeth of a very stiff wind. It was quite a tussle, in which Starker had to take a hand to make any progress at all. He did splendidly and we pulled into Winton about 9:30. Peterson came over with the truck and we warmed up in Ely and caught the 12:45 train back to work.

It has been a memorable trip—maybe the best we ever made—and we have made some that are hard to beat. It is the first trip we have made together since we went to Drummond Island with Dad about 1906 or 1907. How Dad would have loved it! I am reminded of Izaak Walton's terse but loving tribute—'an excellent angler, now with God.'

The Loon Island Decalogue

1. Cuss not thine ancient backlash, for the poor cast we have with us always.
2. When thou risest up to smite a mosquito, hold thy peace and lay thy shirt upon the canopy.
3. Cherish thine hat on the portage, that it may be with thee to the end of thy trip.
4. Stack not tortillas without flour, lest they cleave together and thy brother gather up thereof seven baskets full.
5. If thou wouldst bump the tent in a rainstorm, do it over thine own bed.
6. Six days shalt thou paddle and pack, but on the seventh thou shalt wash thy socks.

7. Covet not thy neighbor's shave, lest thou cast for a trout and be given a pickerel.
8. To him that eats shall be given a pancake, but from him that is always wanting to cook shall be taken away even the one that he hath.
9. An aluminum cup is made for forbearance, and a hot griddle is the trial of a patient man.
10. See not thy brothers' bum cast, and love his campsite as thine own. If there be a rock in the tent, lay thy bed upon it. Ask not for more cheese till thou see if there be any, and peace shall be with thee to the end of thy days.

MISCELLANEOUS OBSERVATIONS

Canoes. Turn over at night to keep out dew, and empty all water at once to avoid taking on weight. Keep paddles and skeg clean of 'feather.' Take off hat and pack down jumpers and all packs in facing a head wind. Have a nose ring for painter and for lining. Don't step on yoke pads; place yoke one rib forward of center of canoe. Carry triangular balloon-silk cloth 5' on each side in bow for sail. Carry line. We had two 16' Racine lightweight, each 72 pounds when dry.

Packs. Don't carry over 60 pounds on a tump, or over 90 pounds in any pack. Kenwood Bags are a little too wide to lie flat crossways. Put extra shirt under shoulder pads for canoe yokes.

Beds and tents. 7' x 9' Silkolene wall tent enough for four people. Should have bobbinet head-canopy to cover upper end of beds, lower edge weighted with shot and tied in with tapes. For summer trip wouldn't take sleeping bags or pockets. One feather or wool quilt plus two double blankets for two people.

Clothing. A jumper that buttons in front, or a heavy coat-shirt, is better than a closed overshirt. One extra pair socks, one extra suit underwear, and one extra kerchief is enough. Extra clothes should be in bag for pillow. No camp or extra shoes are worth their weight. In a rock country have rubber soles on boots—if in wet logs or when trout fishing use new sharp conical hobs.

Miscellaneous. Have several iodine 'vaporoles' in medicine kit, in wooden tubes. Take extra glasses.
Utensils. Heavy skillet with griddle lid pays. By no means forget nippers. No aluminum cups.

Natural History

One Saturday night not long ago, two middle-aged farmers set the alarm clock for a dark hour of what proved to be a snowy, blowy Sunday. Milking over, they jumped into a pick-up and sped for the sand counties of central Wisconsin, a region productive of tax deeds, tamaracks, and wild hay. In the evening they returned with a truck full of young tamarack trees and a heart full of high adventure. The last tree was planted in the home marsh by lantern-light. There was still the milking.

In Wisconsin 'man bites dog' is stale news compared with 'farmer plants tamarack.' Our farmers have been grubbing, burning, draining, and chopping tamarack since 1840. In the region where these farmers live the tree is exterminated. Why then should they want to replace it? Because after twenty years they hope to reintroduce sphagnum moss under the grove, and then lady's-slippers, pitcher plants, and the other nearly extinct wildflowers of the aboriginal Wisconsin bogs.

No extension bureau had offered these farmers any prize for this utterly quixotic undertaking. Certainly no hope of gain motivated it. How then can one interpret its meaning? I call it Revolt—revolt against the tedium of the merely economic

57

attitude toward land. We assume that because we had to sub-
jugate the land to live on it, the best farm is therefore the one
most completely tamed. These two farmers have learned from
experience that the wholly tamed farm offers not only a slender
livelihood but a constricted life. They have caught the idea
that there is pleasure to be had in raising wild crops as well as
tame ones. They propose to devote a little spot of marsh to
growing native wildflowers. Perhaps they wish for their land
what we all wish for our children—not only a chance to make
a living but also a chance to express and develop a rich and
varied assortment of inherent capabilities, both wild and tame.
What better expresses land than the plants that originally grew
on it?

I here talk about the pleasure to be had in wild things, about
natural-history studies as a combination sport and science.

History has not conspired to make my task an easy one. We
naturalists have much to live down. There was a time when
ladies and gentlemen wandered afield not so much to learn
how the world is put together as to gather subject matter for
tea-time conversation. This was the era of dickey-bird ornithology, of botany expressed in bad verse, of ejaculatory vapors
such as 'ain't nature grand.' But if you will scan the amateur
ornithological or botanical journals of today you will see that
a new attitude is abroad. But this is hardly the result of our
present system of formal education.

I know an industrial chemist who spends his spare time re-
constructing the history of the passenger pigeon and its dramatic demise as a member of our fauna. The pigeon became
extinct before this chemist was born, but he has dug up more
knowledge of pigeons than anyone had previously possessed.
How? By reading every newspaper ever printed in our state,
as well as contemporary diaries, letters, and books. I estimate
that he has read 100,000 documents in his search for pigeon

data. This gigantic labor, which would kill any man undertaking it as a task, fills him with the keen delight of a hunter scouring the hills for scarce deer, of an archeologist digging up Egypt for a scarab. And of course such an undertaking re-

quires more than digging. After the scarab is found its interpretation requires the highest skill—a skill not to be learned from others but rather to be developed by the digger as he digs. Here, then, is a man who has found adventure, exploration, science, and sport, all in the back yard of current history, where millions of lesser men find only boredom.

Another exploration—this time literally of a back yard—is a study of the song sparrow conducted by an Ohio housewife. This commonest of birds had been scientifically labeled and classified a hundred years ago, and forthwith forgotten. Our Ohio amateur had the notion that in birds, as in people, there are things to be known over and above name, sex, and clothes. She began trapping the song sparrows in her garden, marking each with a celluloid anklet, and thus she was able to identify each individual by its colored marker, to observe and record their migrations, feedings, fightings, singings, matings, nestings, and deaths; in short, to decipher the inner workings of the sparrow community. In ten years she knew more about sparrow society, sparrow politics, sparrow economics, and sparrow psychology than anyone had ever learned about any bird. Science beat a path to her door. Ornithologists of all nations seek her counsel.

These two amateurs happen to have achieved fame, but no thought of fame motivated their original work. Fame came *ex post facto*. It is not fame, however, that I am talking about. They achieved personal satisfactions which are more important than fame, and hundreds of other amateurs are achieving these satisfactions. I now ask: What is our educational system doing to encourage personal amateur scholarship in the natural-history field? We can perhaps seek an answer to this question by dropping in on a typical class in a typical zoology department. We find there students memorizing the names of the bumps on the bones of a cat. It is important, of course, to study bones; otherwise we should never comprehend the evolutionary process by which animals came into existence. But why memorize the bumps? We are told that this is part of biological discipline. I ask, though, whether a comprehension of the living animal and how it holds its place in the sun is not an equally important part. Unfortunately the living animal is virtually

60

omitted from the present system of zoological education. In my own university, for example, we offer no course in ornithology or mammalogy.

Botanical education is in like case, except perhaps that the displacement of interest in the living flora has been not quite so extreme.

The reasons for this eviction of outdoor studies from the schools goes back into history. Laboratory biology came into existence at about the time when amateur natural history was of the dickey-bird variety, and when professional natural history consisted of labeling species and amassing facts about food habits without interpreting them. In short, a growing and vital laboratory technique was at that time placed in competition with a stagnated outdoor technique. It was quite natural that laboratory biology soon came to be regarded as the superior form of science. As it grew it crowded natural history out of the educational picture.

The present educational marathon in memorizing the geography of bones is the aftermath of this perfectly logical process of competition. It has, of course, other justifications: medical students need it. Zoology teachers need it. But I contend that the average citizen does not need it so badly as he needs some understanding of the living world.

In the interim, field studies have developed techniques and ideas quite as scientific as those of the laboratory. The amateur student is no longer confined to pleasant ambles in the country resulting merely in lists of species, lists of migration dates, and lists of rarities. Bird banding, feather-marking, censusing, and experimental manipulations of behavior and environment are techniques available to all, and they are quantitative science. The amateur can, if he has imagination and persistence, select and solve actual scientific natural-history problems as virgin as the stratosphere.

61

The modern view is to regard laboratory and field not as competitive but rather as complementary studies. Curricula, however, do not yet reflect this new situation. It takes money to enlarge curricula, hence the average college student who inclines toward natural-history avocations is rebuffed rather than encouraged by his university. Instead of being taught to see his native countryside with appreciation and intelligence, he is taught to carve cats. Let him be taught both if this is possible, but if one must be omitted let it be the latter.

To visualize more clearly the lopsidedness and sterility of biological education as a means of building citizens, let's go afield with some typical Phi Beta Kappa student and ask him some questions. We can safely assume he knows how angiosperms and cats are put together, but let us test his comprehension of how the land is put together.

We are driving down a country road in northern Missouri. Here is a farmstead. Look at the trees in the yard and the soil in the field and tell us whether the original settler carved his farm out of prairie or woods. Did he eat prairie chicken or wild turkey for his Thanksgiving? What plants grew here originally which do not grow here now? Why did they disappear? What did the prairie plants have to do with creating the corn-yielding capacity of this soil? Why does this soil erode now but not then?

Again, suppose we are touring the Ozarks. Here is an abandoned field in which the ragweed is sparse and short. Does this tell us anything about why the mortgage was foreclosed? About how long ago? Would this field be a good place to look for quail? Does short ragweed have any connection with the human story behind yonder graveyard? If all the ragweed in this watershed were short, would that tell us anything about the future of floods in the stream? About the future prospects for bass or trout?

I fear that our Phi Beta Kappa biologist would consider these questions insane, but they are not. Any amateur naturalist with a seeing eye should be able to speculate intelligently on all of them, and have a lot of fun doing it. You will see,

too, that modern natural history deals only incidentally with the identity of plants and animals, and only incidentally with their habits and behaviors. It deals principally with their relations to each other, their relation to the soil and water in which they grow, and their relations to the human beings who sing about 'my country' but see little or nothing of its inner workings. This new science of relationships is called ecology, but what we call it matters nothing. The question is, does the educated citizen know he is only a cog in an ecological mechanism? That if he will work with that mechanism his mental wealth and his material wealth can expand indefinitely? But that if he refuses to work with it, it will ultimately grind him to dust? If education does not teach us these things, then what is education for?

Conservationists have, I fear, adopted the pedagogical method of the prophets: we mutter darkly about impending doom if people don't mend their ways. The doom is impending, all right; no one can be an ecologist, even an amateur one, without seeing it. But do people mend their ways for fear of calamity? I doubt it. They are more likely to do it out of pure curiosity and interest. We shall be ready, I think, to practice conservation when 'farmer plants tamarack' is no longer news.

Canada, 1925

A.L., C.S.L., A.S.L., L.B.L.

P. O. Ely, Minn.

8 August, 1925

At 4 p.m. we ended an unsuccessful argument with the aged Skipper of the Winton Launch, during which we tried to induce him to tow us to the railroad portage at the end of Fall Lake. In view of his natural monopoly of this transportation system, Saturday was a poor day to persuade him to make an extra trip. So we piled the outfit into the canoe and started up Fall Lake under our own power. Our outfit consisted of:

1 Peterson Pack containing a blanket, axe, and 75 nominal pounds of chuck, the actual weight of the pack being.........	95 pounds
1 Bed Roll with tumpline, consisting of 6 single blankets, 7 x 9 Silkolene tent, and 2 rods, actual weight	45 "
1 Duffel Bag, with cook kit and miscellaneous tackle	30 "
1 18′ Racine Canoe rated at..........	90 "
TOTAL OUTFIT	260 "

65

Made the five miles to the old log landing in just an hour, all four of us paddling most of the way. Saw several mallards and many campers.

We aspired to camp close to Canada tonight but when the monopolist of the motor portage pulled in, he discovered a shortage of gas, a flat tire, and other appropriate objections to an extra trip on Saturday evening. So we loaded the stuff back in the canoe and pulled over to a pretty rock point and philosophically pitched camp. We called it Flat-tire Camp but enjoyed it, until the wind went down about bedtime and the mosquitoes arrived. We spent the night in guerrilla fighting and at daylight they started a general offensive and routed us out.

9 August

It rained a bit during the night and the morning turned out sparkling cool. Some mallards passed over during breakfast. A launch arrived from Winton before eight and took us across the four-mile portage and on to Bailey Bay west of Prairie Portage. We stopped at the Canadian Ranger Station to get our licenses but nobody home. Henry Chosa, who took us over this portage, is a real character and a good hand. He told us a Minneapolis man was starting to build cottages on the islands of Basswood Lake this fall—so that's the end of the wilderness south of the boundary.

It rained going over the portage from Bailey Bay but we found our outfit carries nicely in a single trip. The lake we came to (Meadow Lake?) runs north for a mile or so and then empties west by a very short portage into another lake, which runs west for a couple of miles and then sharp north. Just after the north turn the wind got so bad we camped.

Previously we had landed on a little island to see if it contained a good camp site and found it loaded with big blueberries. We filled up.

Saw two deer yards in this east arm, where all the shore cedars were trimmed up six feet high.

Tried for fish where the meadow lake stream empties in. Carl hooked a small pike but lost him.

Our new camp is on a windswept rock point. Driving tent pegs, we got all mussed up with blueberry juice.

Near by is the recent sign of a large bear—evidently been eating raspberries and had visited this blueberry island for his dessert.

It is now 4 p.m. and we have camp all made, a kettle of hominy is on the coals, the boys have hung up a bucket of blueberries. All that's lacking is the fish for supper—Carl is out after him.

We don't know what lake we're on, and don't care . . .

Carl later came in with a nice pike—we fried the planks and found it excellent. After supper trolled deep for trout but no strikes. Explored a quiet bay running south. A beaver was swimming around it. Found a plain portage going south and on the other end of it came upon a big water with sawed logs among the driftwood—evidently Basswood Lake. A big red buck was feeding on the shore.

10 August

After a fine blueberry breakfast with loon music we packed up and hit north. Found the outlet—a little marshy river in which were a dozen big black mallards. This took us to a small lake full of water lilies, which we called the Pike Pond because it was full of small pike. Down the river we found it lost under big boulders but portaged to a big lake near by. Saw a camp on it with four people—on asking them we found that we were in North Bay. So we cut east to a stream coming out of the Shade Lake chain. At the portage at the head of this stream we bumped into Carl's friend Jim Harper and Mrs. Harper, just coming out. Had lunch with them.

Went on through a series of beaver-flooded lakes—South, Center, North, and into Shade Lake. Camped in a little bay in the east end of Shade. Right now we are having a time catching fish for supper—there are small bass here but we can't get any strikes.

There are entirely too many signs of old camps here—even a big crop of regular houseflies. A flock of fine black mallards passing over at sunset helped crystallize our desire to strike off into unfrequented country.

11 August

After a comfortable night, we set off to the north. The sun was just dispersing a soft fog when we carried down into Tray Lake—a fine little white water unspoiled by beaver-flooding. Here we tried for both bass and trout but couldn't raise anything. Then came a long portage into Cray Lake. Just as Carl and I arrived at the end of the portage Starker and Luna set up a shout from a near-by point—they had hooked a fine bass and we all went over to help land him. We all voted to camp here and have some fishing. Found a fine place on the north shore. While Carl and I were doing some chores Starker and Luna set off on a little fishing trip and came back with four fine bass. We then had a swim and some lunch and a nap, and picked a mess of blueberries. There was bear sign in the berry patch. In the evening after a bass dinner we all turned out for a fishing spree. None of us has ever experienced such bass fishing. Three times two of us had bass jumping out and shaking the hook simultaneously. We all caught bass till our arms were tired. They struck best between sunset and dusk. They were lying in the old beaver-flooded timber along the shore. We put them all back. This would be a glorious fly-fishing lake. We found our scales would not weigh the small fish, of which we caught many that do not show on the record.

Twice we jumped black mallards from up on the bank, each time in the vicinity of blueberry bushes. Next day on Yum-Yum Lake we practically proved they were after berries when we twice jumped them from the face of steep rocks thirty feet above water and covered with blueberry bushes. After all, how foolish they would be not to eat these fine dew-covered berries dangling from every bank!

12 August

After a very early breakfast we turned out for a last round with the bass. We repeated last night's performance and had a hilarious time. Put them all back.

Packed up and portaged over a little-used trail full of moose sign into Little Tray Lake. Saw bass jumping here but did not stop to fish. Then over a short portage into a lily-covered river which emptied into an arm of Yum-Yum. After trolling unsuccessfully and exploring the various arms of the lake we camped on a fine gently sloping granite point and then set out in earnest for trout. Put the copper line (about 150 feet) on top of the silk casting line and weighted it with an ordinary large sinker. This let out at an angle of about 30° from horizontal in slow paddling and gave us good depth. In the mouth of the arm from which the portage comes I hooked a fine fish. We were surprised at the lively action of the copper line. When he was in sight we found he was a fine trout. By towing him we played him out without making any sharp angles between the rod and the line. He proved to be a fine 3½ pounds.

We made tracks for camp and fried him, with macaroni as a side dish. As we were washing dishes we saw big splashes on the opposite shore and thought it was a moose. Soon we realized, however, that the splashes were beaver. Carl now gave the fish a round. Caught a pike—we never suspected they got down so deep. Next Carl set another fish which proved to be a big trout. We hung him up and turned in, to the patter of rain, all of us dog tired and I with some rheumatism in one shoulder and ribs where I fell on a snag the other day. Beaver splashed around as we went to sleep.

13 August

Slept late, breakfasting luxuriously in a cool breeze at 6:30. Chored around camp for a while and now are all set for a day's excursion into Kashahpi Lake.

At the outlet of the lake we found an entrancing rocky glen with a deep pool covered with multicolored water-lily leaves. Pale birches and blueberries overhung the mossy banks, and just below the stream gurgled down a cascade of boulders. Overhead hung a great cliff with colored lichens and gnarled pines and cedars. It was quite the loveliest spot I have ever seen. I attempted some pictures but they probably will not do it justice without the colors.

We found the portage to be a very old unimproved route blockaded by three beaver ponds and flanked by frequent muskegs under high cliffs. It was much harder going afoot than it would have been by canoe. The direction is west, not south as shown on the map, and the distance is much greater than the map shows. At noon, having not yet reached the lake, we attempted to cut across country westward, but found ourselves in a seemingly endless succession of spruce swamps and granite knolls covered with scrubby pine and blueberries. So we struck back to the lower beaver pond and had lunch and a nap, first, however, filling up on blueberries, which were extra large and sweet.

This whole country is covered with moose and deer sign, but we saw no evidence of grouse. The moose seem to browse the shoots of alder, willow, and moosewood maple. There were beds in the tall grass bordering the muskeg. Beaver trails led up into the woods everywhere, and in the ponds were big lodges so old as to be covered with grass. A flock of grown but flightless black mallards swam around in the ponds accompanied and led by a single merganser.

Carl knocked a squirrel out of a tree with his slingshot but he was not hit squarely and got away. He hit him second shot at twenty yards, indicating that the slingshots may be pretty effective pot-boilers. We brought clay marbles for ammunition.

This river, where it leaves Yum-Yum, is in a narrow gorge and seemingly easily dammed. Why then have the beavers not raised the whole lake as in the case of Cray, Shade, et cetera? Carl suggests that the very narrowness of the outlet would cause floods to tear out the dam. If this is the case, the beaver seeks the wide dam site, not the narrow one. It will be interesting to observe how this hypothesis works out.

Coming back in the canoe, Luna trolled with the copper line and landed a fine trout well down in the bay. We turned him loose, already having a sack of planked trout steak hung in a tree at camp.

After a supper of trout chowder with bannocks, we had a pleasant evening listening to the loons and splashing of beaver. Luna caught a pike right by the campfire. The pike were working on minnows gathered around some rice we had spilled in the water.

Forgot to wind my watch yesterday so had to set my watch by guess, hereinafter known as Yum-Yum Meridian.

Argued till bedtime about whether to risk the venture into Kashahpiwigamak or to return by the safe and sane Dell Lake chain into North Bay. Being well fed and full of courage we passed an order in council to return via Kashahpi. The big gamble is the negotiability of the long portage from the south-west arm of Kashahpi into Rock Lake. We shall see!

14 August

Up before sun-up. A soft fog on the lake—much loon music— a beaver cutting a wide circle around the fire as he wended his way lodge-ward for his day's rest. Carl and I flipped flapjacks and then tried to wake the boys. They wouldn't budge until we told Luna there was a jar of jam open, and Starker that a shoal of minnows had gathered and were doubtless followed by an escort of pike. Thereupon they came a-running.

1:00 p.m. (Yum-Yum Meridian). We are back at the Lily pool on Yum-Yum. We started down the outlet about seven this morning, cutting our own portages into the first two beaver ponds and sliding the canoe over six other dams. We got well below yesterday's explorations but still no Kashahpi, while Carl went down a mile and climbed a high cliff from where he could see the river for several miles more but no lake. More-over it runs straight south while the map has it heading nearly north.

This country down the river is full of moose sign but the beaver workings are much older than those above—in fact we found old dams from which all wood had rotted entirely away. They were covered with grass and the floods had torn spillways through them.

On the lowest pond reached with the canoe we flushed a pair of widgeons. Saw our black ducks again. I killed a squirrel with the rubber gun, hitting him in the head, second shot, at 25 feet.

On our way back up the now familiar Yum-Yum we took a second look at the northwest bay just to satisfy our curiosity about the whereabouts of the elusive Kashahpi portage. We

didn't think it probable that Yum-Yum would have two out-
lets, yet the direction of Widgeon River was so at variance
with the map that something seemed wrong. Sure enough, at
the bottom of the northwest bay was a blazed white pine and a
plain trail headed north. We had missed it entirely on our first
exploration because we were looking for a portage *down an
outlet* stream, whereas this trail *ran up a hill*. This error was
natural enough. The real greenhorn performance was in not
smelling a rat sooner on the wrong direction of the Widgeon
River.

We walked over the newly found portage just to make sure.
It runs through several upland muskegs and alder swamps
which must be pretty soft during a wet season but otherwise
it is an easy route through beautiful shady woods. It emerges
on a little arm of Kashahpi, affording a calm easy landing.
The rest of the shore in sight was steep cliffs.

There were lots of moose and deer sign on the portage.
Coming back a snowshoe rabbit hopped across the trail and
stopped in the alders about 25 feet distant. We all popped at
him with our slingshots. At the second shot I hit him behind
the ear with a marble and knocked him cold. It was such a
funny performance to kill a rabbit with a rubber gun that we
all roared with laughter.

Soon after a cock partridge hopped out of the trail—the
only one seen thus far on the trip. We popped several marbles
at him but failed to hit. The grouse seem to have reared no
broods this year.

Starker picked up a big pike in Yum-Yum on our way back.
Portaged into Leg and Cray and camped at our bass grounds,
feeling very much at home in our old camp. A partridge flew
across the lake to the high hill opposite camp as we were cooking supper. Dined on a gallon of bean soup stocked with ham
and squirrel. It was delicious. We slept the sleep of the just

after a very satisfying failure to camp on the elusive Kashahpi. Moral: Look at your compass hard and often, and if the country doesn't agree with the map find out who's a liar and why.

15 August

As I sit against a mossy rock writing up the sequel to yesterday's adventures, a cool breeze fans the blueberry bushes, which dangle big dewy fruit over the very page of this journal.

74

Starker and Luna, after being prodded through the job of dishes and beds, are organizing the fishing tackle for the day with thoroughness and enthusiasm. Carl is trying a new way of putting the tumpline on the boys' packs. Gentle waves are lapping the canoe in invitation for the day's travel. Down the lake a loon calls, and back in the aspens a pine squirrel tells us to get the hell out o' here. We will!

Only a few strikes as we tried the bass on the way out. Stopped at Dell Lake and caught several bass and a dozen perch on an improvised bait made out of a small hook, a piece of perch belly, a red rag, and a nail. After we had cleaned the perch for lunch we found the flesh full of encysted parasites; had to throw the fish away.

Came through to Lily Lake via Wolf Lake. Camped on a fine shelving rock carpeted with wintergreen and moss, where we had a fine swim, a superlative lunch, and a nap with a good many flies.

On down to North Bay by way of a pretty lily-padded stream, the banks of which were tramped down by deer and moose tracks. Found a stiff head wind blowing up Basswood so we decided to take the inside passage on the west side of the bay. We found this very interesting country; there are pretty camp sites on smooth shelving rock points, with deep bays full of green grass and lily pads. At the portage of the inside passage a doe and her yearling were browsing pads. The wind blew in our faces, so we were able, by keeping quiet when her head was up, to paddle up within 25 feet. Then she got our wind and got out with a snort and a bound, Carl snapping her broadside before she disappeared in the brush. We had got between the doe and the yearling and they had a lot of whistling and hesitating to do back in the brush before they finally got together again.

At the end of the passage we bucked a mile of head wind

across the open bay, camping on a lovely pine point on the east shore. A flock of black ducks flushed from the lee of the point as we landed, and we later found all the blueberries cleaned up from the open ground near the shore.

This was quite the prettiest camp we have had. The rocks form a fine fireplace, tables, easy chairs, and landing, while a flat rock in an opening is covered with deep dry moss and duff forming a ready-made bed. The whole point is covered with blueberries. An International Boundary post, set in the rock, came very near being in the right position to use as a tent peg. We lived high on fried pike steaks and creamed macaroni with cheese, and turned in at ten after a delightful day, all a little blue at the prospect of tomorrow's departure for the land of neckties and boiled shirts.

16 August

Up at 3:30 (Yum-Yum Meridian; we afterward found Central Time to be an hour fast) and got under way at 5:30—a tolerably good start. Several of our black ducks came back to their little bay as we ate breakfast. It was cloudy and threatening rain so we missed the chance to take pictures of this especially pretty camp. Arrived at the Ranger Station at 7:00 Yum-Yum (8:00 Central) and paid for our licenses. Heading on up the bay toward Four Mile Portage we saw a launch, and hailing it, found it headed for Winton, so we hopped aboard.

Reunion

A.L., C.S.L., F.L.

---

15 November, 1925
Cold, cloudy, NW wind
New wet snow
Near Stroughurst, Ill.

This was more nearly goose than quail weather, but after sixteen bobwhiteless years even a bad day was welcome. Incidentally, this was the first time the three of us had ever been on a quail hunt all together.

Evidently because of the weather conditions, all the birds were bushed up under hedges, grape tangles, and similar spots of bare ground. We didn't find a covey in the corn and saw only one track in the snow, and that one was made after we had started a covey to run away down a fence line. Several of the coveys rose wild, especially before getting thoroughly scattered, and our cold feet made good shooting difficult.

Flick did pretty well, considering his unorthodox education on the western running birds. He made only one firm point on a covey but many on singles, and he did no precipitate flushing even on running bunches. One noticeable fact was that even Flick found none of the singles that flew off with hanging legs,

77

although we searched hard for them. Evidently they lie very close. Between us there were three or four of these. We also lost several birds that came down straight but were evidently winged and did some hard running.

We scattered the first covey down a hedge and had some comparatively easy shooting. We then drew a blank on several pretty coverts, but found a second bunch in a crab thicket roofed over with a grape-vine tangle. These scattered nicely in the corn but somehow we didn't punch them much. On this bunch I made an exceptionally long kill on a towering single but couldn't find him.

In the same locust patch we found a covey of two-thirds-grown birds, which we didn't follow very hard because of their small size. This is not very logical, of course. It would have been better to let the big strong birds off easy and harvest the little ones, which had a lesser chance of getting through the winter.

By this time it was noon and our feet were in pretty cold storage so we found a dryish place under a box-elder tree, shed our boots, and took on some broiled pork chops and toast. There was more comfort than propriety about this camp, the fire being surrounded by concentric rings of the following:

First: Pork chops broiling and sizzling on sticks
Second: Toast, browning ditto
Third: Socks, steaming ditto
Fourth: Boots, likewise steaming
Fifth: Feet, not only steaming but aching like a newly pulled tooth
Sixth: Hunters and dogs

After we took on the chops and partly dried footwear it was amusing with what circumspection we went about the old job of knocking wet snow off the brush and weeds. We hit off into new territory and very promptly two big coveys flushed wild and scattered into a woodlot. We got rid of a lot of shells here without hurting the birds very much, partly because most of the birds would not lie and the singles ran badly after scattering. We put more shot into the tree trunks than into the quail.

Proceeding car-ward, Flick located a very large covey which we saw on the ground under a heavy grape tangle but never succeeded in wholly flushing. We got only one bird out of this whole layout.

Almost immediately afterward got out a nice covey which flew into posted land, but we got two that headed back toward open territory. By now it was pretty dark, and we went back to the car, first having an unpleasant argument with the owner of said posted land who thought we had purposely skirted his fence to steal his birds.

On our way out at sunset we saw a beautiful bunch sail with bowed wings into the jack oaks, evidently having flown down from the hills for roosting in the extensive jack-oak coverts.

All day long we saw cat tracks and I think one fox track. Saw one very large horned owl. Many cardinals.

I think there is no solution for this posted-land problem except private leases. I am surprised and reassured at the number of coveys per farm. A couple of farms now raise 6–8 coveys—enough for two men—and with reasonable preservation of coverts the number of coveys could be increased.

P.S. I asked the boys if the bittersweet berry is eaten by wildlife. They say cedar waxwings once worked on one of the vines in the yard.

Red Fox Day

A.L., C.S.L.

---

16 November, 1925
Cloudy, cool, W breeze
2–4:30 p.m.
Bluffs N. of Hopper, Ill.

We had hardly left the car at the foot of the bluff when we heard Flick put up quail out of a thicket of saplings on the bank of Allison Creek. Possibly they flushed wild. Carl guessed they would scale the bluff so we started up and soon put up a pair. I was standing on one leg and missed with the right and probably with the left, too, but Carl in any event got the second one.

We skirted the edge of the bluff into the Allison canyons and I noticed a freshly dug den in the hillside. A few yards farther, as I rounded the point of a hogback, a big fiery-red fox darted out of the cover of a fallen limb in the bottom of the draw and started up the opposite slope. I shot about fifteen yards from the place he started. He slipped for an instant and then turned at right angles along the slope and got behind a tree before I could fire the other barrel.

Carl meanwhile was standing on top of the hill, where he

could see the whole performance, but being some 10 yards farther from the fox than I was, and with brush in the way, he couldn't shoot to advantage.

Flick, when the fox jumped, was below and behind me but saw him instantly and was soon dashing after him, not returning for a long time. Once we thought we heard him bark and

we ran forward, but it proved to be a dog in a farmyard below us. The fox was going strong at 150 yards so I don't think he was seriously hurt.

Foxy thoughts (ex post facto, but not post mortem)

I was shooting 2¾" 1 oz. 7½ c. shot. With such small shot, shooting virtually into his back muscles, the ribs protected by a long angle through the fur, I should have realized that the only chance I had was to deliver such a shock as to knock him over and thus gain time enough to slip in a #4 or #6 load, both of which I had in my shell vest. Realizing this, I should have pulled both triggers at once at the earliest possible instant. This might have given Flick time to rush in and hold him. I was, as a matter of fact, so dazed by the fact of seeing a fox at all that I shot an instant slower than I would have shot at a quail.

Evidently what happened was that the fox was at work on his den as we came up. He tried to sneak over the hogback and up the draw to get away from me, but seeing Carl on top he squatted under the fallen limb, but had to get out as I rounded the hogback.

Well, anyhow, the whole episode shows how much excitement a fox can cause by simply carrying away a few birdshot. If we had hung up his hide we should have put on a war dance the rest of the afternoon. He was in magnificent feather and seemed over four feet long over-all.

Seeing foxes under every bush, we proceeded on our quail hunt. Put up a big covey in the corn on top of a hill with a deserted farmhouse and orchard on it. We couldn't see them alight because they flew south over the crest of the hill, and we spent a long time trying to find them. We finally found they were scattered in the corn around a little pothole but were lying so close that they had to be stepped on before they would get out. The corn was tall and ungathered and hard to shoot in but we managed to garner three birds.

Coming home at night Flick again flushed four birds from the thicket at the car and they towered up the bluff over Carl's head, but we didn't see them in time to shoot.

Still seeing and talking red, we mushed home through the deep mud after one of those brave adventurous days that we shall smoke pipes over in our old age.

Current River, 1926

A.L., C.S.L., F.L.

P. O. Van Buren, Mo.

26 November

Met Carl and Fritz in St. Louis 11 a.m. A cold windy day, gradually clearing up. Reached Leeper 9 p.m. and stayed at Ozark Hotel.

27 November

Arrived Van Buren 9 a.m. and hit the river at 10:30. A fine sunny morning. The river is very fast for a mile or so below town, then calms down somewhat. About noon we had our first excitement when 30 mallards came up the river and began to circle the timber a hundred yards to our left, settling down in a little backwater. We sneaked them, only I going all the way. I got within 30 yards but got only one on the rise; alibi: dark background and brush. They circled and came over us. Everybody missed; alibi: too far. Just as we were leaving five came back, but seeing our boat they went on. We landed again to wait when eight got out unexpectedly below us, one big drake passing within easy range of Carl and me. Alibi: none. We named this Bungle Bay.

Fritz later killed a green-wing that flushed from the bank.

Camped in time for a little quail hunt. Found a small covey in a cornfield and got four. I killed a huge rabbit going home. We had quail and sweet potatoes—not a bad first-night supper, and spent a comfortable night. This camp was full of a dry weed whose pods tinkled as one walked through.

28 November

Up before daylight. No mishap except that tinkleweed seed got in the coffee. Hit the river about 8:00, stopping here and there to hunt quail. Found two coveys and did well on them, nine altogether. Both were in the corn. Killed two bluebills (singles) in the river. Camped shortly after noon in a protected cove.

Got camp all dolled up. Carl and Fritz then prospected for turkey while I got dinner. The boys report the hills are burned and flinty. Had a comfortable evening, with music and walnuts by the fire. During the night we had a sharp shower that sprayed through the lean-to and got Fritz's bed wet. We had put up the tent so the outfit kept dry.

29 November

Cooked coffeecake before daylight and made an early start for a turkey trip across the creek. Hunted westerly for about three miles, getting into better and less burned country with red-haws in the bottoms. No turkey sign. A razorback sow charged Flick when he eyed her offspring too closely. Ate lunch on a high hill and took a little nap in a sunny place. Then went north a mile and thence easterly down a beautiful valley with haws and an incredible crop of thick-shelled hickory nuts and fat squirrels, of which Carl killed one who stuck his chin up between a tree fork. He tipped him so lightly that we had a foot race when he fell. Here, just as we got into ideal turkey country, we again struck farms. Flick flushed a covey of quail on which Fritz made a double. Killed four altogether.

Back at the Hornet Nest Spring we had seen another covey with two hawks in attendance—a sharpshin and a cooper. Did not shoot here as we suspected turkey.

It was a long jog back to the river, which we struck at the 'villa,' and we had to skirt a bluff to get down to the boat. Coon sign (either pokeberries or black-gum berries) on a bayou. The soil in the cornfields makes very heavy going after the rain.

We came into camp all fagged out but soon recovered after a monumental dinner. We started with a mallard, a teal, and a big pot of mashed potatoes, but this leaving a vacancy, we roasted three quail to boot, and then ate walnuts for an hour before we were finally chock-a-block.

The quail we cleaned tonight had whole corn, seeds about radish size, and green leaves (probably oxalis, which is abundant in the cornfields) in the crops.

Had a comfortable night in spite of a sharp frost.

30 November

A hominy omelet before daylight is a good start toward a fine day. After breakfast we dolled up our faces, washed handkerchiefs, and made a leisurely start. A fine sunny day to drift down the river. Ate lunch in a marvelously pretty cutoff with a deep blue-green current flowing under an avenue of stately sycamores. We sat in the sun on a little bench and took a nap and then moved on, in spite of the temptation to stop and camp. Taking a little quail hunt in a big bottom on the east side, Fritz found a persimmon tree and we spent half an hour clubbing 'simmons' and spitting seeds. Toward evening we had difficulty in finding a camp site that combined wood, dryness, shelter, privacy, fishing hole, boat landing, quail and turkey ground. It was dark before we finally found a suitable place under a huge leaning sycamore, to which we pitched the lean-to. Luckily we had bean soup already cooked. We ate an even gallon of it and went to bed.

1 December

After breakfast we idled around an hour setting fish lines and getting up oak wood. Another fine sunny day, the threatened rain having passed by. Caught a hideous waterdog on one line almost as soon as we had set it. There was another one on it in the evening.

Went on a quail hunt in the corn surrounding our woods. Found only one covey. Shot rather badly in spite of the fact that they scattered in a coral-berry bottom. One field through which we passed was lined with walnut trees with incredible supplies of big nuts lying in the corn furrows. Also found a few butternuts.

After a rabbit soup by Carl (excellent, by the way, mixed with Julienne and noodles) we crossed the river and after setting a trap went on a quail hunt. Found a covey of fifteen. They scattered in an oak thicket and we didn't shine at all in getting them out, especially after Flick got excited about a rabbit nearly as big as himself and flushed several birds wild. Then went up the hollow prospecting for turkeys but found no sign. Coming back we picked up a dozen sweet turnips from a patch planted in the corn.

We had set sourdough at noon and this evening had the finest loaf of hot bread one could imagine, together with broiled bluebills and fried yams. What one can cook on these oak coals is almost unbelievable. This was a cold night but we weathered it nicely with the help of a cane bed Fritz had built.

2 December

Again made a leisurely start, partly because of needed sock washing, shoe greasing, etc., and partly because it was frosty cold. We dislike to leave our old sycamore.

Stopped at an uninhabited cornfield on the east bank and soon flushed a big covey of fifteen (most coveys here are small, even where unshot). They flew almost into my face and I was so rattled that I only slobbered one instead of making an easy double. They disappeared over a slight rise in the corn. In spite of an hour's hunting we found only one scattered bird, which Carl hit as he climbed the timber on the bluff, and the bird dropped against a limestone cliff. Flick and Carl did some alpine stuff in retrieving him.

Went on down the river and soon came to the mouth of the

Buffalo Fork. Took a walk up to explore for camps. Flick flushed a small covey in the cane on the edge of the corn and Carl and I each got one of the scatters.

Decided to push up the Buffalo to a nice camp about a half mile up. Had to climb over a sycamore snag as we pushed the boat under, just as we did on the Rillito in the Gulf of the Colorado. At the head of navigation we made a magnificent camp, including a table made of a single slab of lightning-riven white oak two feet wide and five long. Cut two backloads of cane for a bed. Had a dinner of roast quail, and noodles with 'crachelchen' made of Swede bread. They are infinitely better than ordinary croutons. Set the traps before supper.

3 December

Cornbread and syrup for breakfast. Shaved and hung out the bedding and got dolled up generally. Some coon hunters came by at daylight and said there were turkey in the ridges back of camp so we renewed our turkey zeal and hit the flints.

Hunted up a draw of Buffalo Creek running southeast. The lower part of it was full of gray squirrels. These are smaller and the fox squirrels and rabbits larger than I have ever seen. This draw looked very good, the day was sunny and fine, and still-hunting through the woods was a keen pleasure in spite of the absence of turkeys. Once a crow gave me palpitations by cawing like a gobbler.

We met on the main ridge at the head of the draw and lunched on roast quail under a hickory tree full of fine nuts, of which we ate a large bait. Thence westerly along the ridge and hunted down another draw which opened into some old fields full of springs and surrounded by laden haw trees. It looked good enough to make a turkey's mouth water but there was no sign.

Thence down the main creek hunting quail. After Carl and

88

CURRENT RIVER, 1926

I had cut for camp Fritz found a big covey and killed three, including a double on the rise, but he lost two because the place was full of cockleburs and Flick wouldn't work.

A wonderful dinner of squirrel Julienne with a big loaf of hot sourdough that had raised the lid of the dutch oven during the day and spilled dough (which we fried for Flick).

A warm night, and we made the most of it in beds just in from the warm sun. Coon hunters and their hounds serenaded most of the night.

4 December

A balmy dawn. The Carolina wrens are singing as I write up yesterday's and speculate upon today's events. I think we shall have a storm. Fritz does, too, as he is rustling extra wood and stowing away clothes from the clothesline.

I slipped off the 'wharf' this morning while washing in the creek and now write barefoot in perfect comfort. That's how warm it is.

Made a grand quail hunt today. Found four coveys, two of them small or remnants of normal-size coveys. We shot badly and lost several down birds due to Flick's getting so tied up with cockleburs that he gave up and couldn't smell.

We found the birds mostly in the corn, the burrier the better. Later in the day they are in the cane fringes or heavy weed patches. They do not frequent the light weed patches or grass as they do farther north.

Flick caught a rabbit today all on his own. We were looking for a cripple in a cane patch when Flick made a plunge and we thought he had our bird, but he came out proudly holding aloft a kicking bunny.

As we were eating supper two horned owls tuned up within gunshot of camp. One had a distinctly deeper voice than the other. They moved about a great deal from tree to tree. It was

89

a thrilling sight to see one swoop down off the hill against the gray afterglow.

A warm night, threatening rain.

5 December

Up at 5:30 and through breakfast by gray of dawn. I lifted the traps while the boys packed up camp. Our baggage has a shrunken look after three days' feasting at our puncheon table.

Made about eight miles down the river with a north wind behind us. There is much wide still water in this section which must be paddled. Tried one cornfield on the east bank but found only a single scattered bird. Began to meet people in this section, including one Current River 'Steamboat' with a stern wheel.

Camped on a high sandy bottom in tall oak and sycamore timber and in half an hour rigged up a fine camp, including a cane bed. This cane makes excellent bedding if laid butts-down, parallel with the length of the bed. It has a faint fragrance that is very agreeable.

After a snack of lunch we found a covey in a ragweed patch within 150 yards of camp and got four birds on the rise, losing a fifth down a possum hole. Flick made a brilliant find on one cripple which had crawled under a pile of driftwood within two feet of a dead bird we had already picked up. Flick worked much better after a greasing of his under parts last night. He is rubbed pretty raw by the weeds and burrs. I got a scatter from this covey.

We next jumped a covey in a high woods undergrown with cane. These scatters were the hardest flyers I have ever seen. They would go up like a skyrocket to the very tops of the trees and then as suddenly pitch down into the cane again. We must have burned half a box of shells on this covey with only one kill by Carl.

Had roast rabbit (Flick's) and macaroni for supper and spent a pleasant evening recounting past adventures on the Colorado delta. A bit of rain during the night but cold again by morning.

6 December

Our last day of hunting. All shaved in the hope of improving our shooting a bit. It is cool and cloudy.

Tried the quail above camp on the west bank. Found the canebrake covey and did a little better with them, getting three. Hunted a lot of new country that looked ideal but found no birds. Saw a large flock of doves but couldn't get near them. Coming back I unexpectedly flushed a big mallard drake out of the head of the buckbrush lake. I shot through some saplings at him but failed to connect. This is the first mallard we have seen since leaving the cove camp.

In the afternoon we crossed the river and while we were cutting mistletoe for the girls, Flick put up a beautiful covey out of the tinkleweeds but nobody had a loaded gun. We got two, however, out of a belated rise and later a couple of scatters.

Next hunted some lovely ragweed patches to the south and found a nice covey. Had a hard time finding them again because we overestimated the distance they flew. Finally got them out. Carl put five right over Fritz and me and we scored four clean misses overhead as they pitched down into the cane. Later we retrieved our reputation a bit by killing some singles. It now began to rain and we regretfully left the whistling birds behind us as we hit for camp.

7 December

A sad morning packing up and wrestling with temptation to hunt another day. Carl smoked his last 'Philadelphia Bayuk,'

91

I nailed a pair of worn-out pants to an oak tree, and Fritz packed up his favorite dish mop as parting ceremonies to mark the end of a famous trip. I sit here on the cane bed, the stripped camp around me and the boys waiting to be off, while the pileated taps an oak limb and the last oak coals of our last camp smoke faintly and die away.

Providentially, it rained all the way down the river to Doniphan, taking some of the edge off our desire to be hunting instead of leaving.

MISCELLANEOUS OBSERVATIONS
CURRENT RIVER TRIP—1926

Tame squirrels. The big fox squirrels are indifferent to one's noisy approach through the dry leaves. Carl suggests this is because the squirrels and the pigs both live in the same places (namely, the hickory groves) and they are accustomed to hearing pigs rustling around all day. We seldom saw fox and gray squirrels on the same ground.

Sexes in quail. Of 18 birds in camp on 4 December, only seven were cocks. It is rather noticeable that one kills more hens than cocks. Of seven additional birds killed 4 December, five were cocks. Four of these cocks were from one covey.

Canebrakes. Cane does not grow at Van Buren but increases gradually in abundance as one goes down the river. It occurs only in fields that are fenced against hogs during the growing season. Usually this means that it is confined to the wooded edges of fields and to the riverbank. The line of demarcation between the fenced and unfenced ground is always sharp.

Nuts. Even the thickest shelled hickories seem to be eaten by hogs, but the walnuts are untouched, evidently because of the unsavory hulls. Squirrels get at the kernels of butternuts by gnawing into the ends and then scooping. The big-nut hickory nuts remaining on the ground at this season are all wormy or empty. How the hogs and squirrels distinguish the poor nuts is a mystery.

Mistletoe is confined almost entirely to the riverbank, the running water evidently ameliorating the winter cold. Fritz saw one bunch in the hills near Doniphan.

Habits of quail. Quail do not seem to use short grass or weeds, even when available. Coveys found in the morning are usually in the corn; those in the afternoon are usually in the cane or ragweed or occasionally in the tinkleweed bottoms. When flushed most coveys go either to the cane or to the wooded bluffs. Scatters in timber often skyrocket to the tops of the trees and then pitch down again, when it would be entirely practicable for them to fly through the timber.

The Lily

This pretty river must have been named by some person other than the usual trader or surveyor, and for some reason other than the gross and obvious one that there are lilies in it—for there are none.

The Lily must have been named by some poet-voyager, and for some more subtle and potent reason—the chance thought, for instance, that not even the wolf in all his glory is yet arrayed as one of these.

Our poet must have discerned the changeful moods that would have forever mocked the giver of a masculine name to this river. You may come upon her at some dancing shingle where irises and marigolds grow on little mossy islands, and nodding willows dip their branches from wide banks. But within the space of three casts you have passed into a long cool corridor where the current runs swift and dark and deep between the roots of alders and ferns, with here and there a spruce solemnly contemplating your not very solemn attempts to cast a fly. Soon you emerge upon a long pool curving in a wide trouty sweep upon a fallen balsam. What a line you could lay upon that pool, did not the balsam prevent your laying any line at all! Of course you could fish it downstream, but somehow you feel as if that would dampen the gay humor that filled the balsam in its particular place.

The pool gives upon another shingle, on which you may cast high, wide, and handsome, but from which the Lily—except on certain rare and unpredictable evenings—withholds her trout.

One wonders what were the Lily's moods before they took her pines. A dark glory they must have been, in the clearing below the Big Pool—there are stumps which our voyager could barely have spanned with two lengths of his rifle. What domes those mighty columns must have held against the sky, to be reflected in the Lily! The pines are gone now, but bobolinks hover over their blackened stumps and praise the bluegrass that has taken their place. Odd it is that birds, and rivers, should know what people don't—that bluegrass is the most praiseworthy thing that the white man has brought into this land; the thing that comes nearest to atoning for what he has taken away.

The Lily chooses her birds well. In the cool dawn a hundred white-throats lament in minor chorus that as yet undiscovered tragedy that broke the heart of 'poor Canada.' An occasional winter wren breaks in upon them with so jovial a whistle that one is led to think perhaps Canada after all has outgrown her secret sorrow. During the day's fishing, anxious mother grouse cluck to their hidden broods and red-wings extoll the lush greenness of the little marshes along the Lily's banks. Not until the last evening light is upon the aspens do the thrushes begin. This is also the hour when fishermen go to sleep. The ringing cadences are clear at first, then dimmer with the waning sunset, until at last the windings and unwindings of thrushes' song merge with the windings and unwindings of the Lily and the long lines that fall unerringly upon her trouty pools in fishermen's dreams.

The Gila, 1927

A.L., HOWARD WEISS

P. O. Glenwood, N. M.

9 November

Left N-Bar Ranch with two packs at 9 a.m. Emil Tipton came with us to take back the stock. Rode down Snow Creek to its mouth, where we passed the last autos. A boy on the Middle Fork below Snow Creek had a fine mess of trout up to 9 inches in length. Saw turkey scratchings near the Trotter place. Arrived at the old Flying V ranch, which Tipton said was the mouth of Canyon Creek, about 2:30, and camped on a watercress spring under two big pines in a little side canyon just north of the old ranch. After lunch Tipton started back with all but one horse while Howard and I spent the rest of the day making camp. Wood scarce, due no doubt to the old ranch.

10 November

Up before daylight just at moonset. Got started before sun-up. Climbed a high point in the little draw back of camp and made a drive along a nice-looking rim but saw no deer and little sign. Concluded that the absence of piñon had caused the deer to move out so we headed east for a high hill that showed piñon through the glasses. Found the true Canyon Creek in a 600-foot gulch just west of the hill. Boiled tea at the bottom of this gulch. Climbing the other side we promptly began to see lots of deer sign. On a high juniper mesa leading up to the hill we saw that the deer had nearly finished the piñons and were feeding heavily on alligator juniper berries. Made a drive of the rincon on the west side of this juniper hill. There was a strong SW wind which was very favorable. I jumped a yearling which almost ran Howard down. Then in a piñon thicket I jumped three very fat does, one of which, I found later by the tracks, had fawns. All these deer that had a chance jumped into the wind rather than up the hill.

A 4 p.m. headed down Canyon Creek for camp. Ran into ten deer going to water and feeding on sage in the creek bottom. Could see no horns, but it was a pretty sight.

An Abert squirrel nearly ran into me while we were watching these deer. He was in black phase.

Did not get to the mouth of Canyon Creek till dark. We thought camp was only a mile or two up the Middle Fork but we encountered a seemingly endless maze of box canyons and S turns in the river. By half past seven we were both pretty nearly all in, and wet from innumerable fordings of the river, so we stopped and boiled some hot water with the sugar left over from lunch. Finally got to camp at 9 p.m. after 3½ hours of steady walking up the Gila. Several deer snorted at us on our way. It was black as pitch till the moon came up about 8:30. Too tired to eat, so we rolled in.

11 November

Spent the morning rustling wood and fixing up around camp, shaving, laundering, and resting from last night's misadventure. At noon made some tea and took a walk—Howard down the canyon and I to the hills south of the river. Found three

97

squirrels eating Douglas Fir cones in one tree and tried to get one by shooting straight up with a blunt arrow. Shot too well, as I had to leave an arrow sticking in a limb. The squirrel

trotted out his whole collection of profanity and kept it up till I was out of sight.

Found a nice-looking juniper mesa with an oak slope below, but there were no berries and little deer sign except whitetail. Started back too late and got tangled in a rimrock near camp. Howard reported seeing nothing except some turkey scratchings.

12 November

Started early for Canyon Creek, laying out a 'baseline' due east from the old Flying V dugway that climbs out back of camp. Hit Canyon Creek a little south of where we climbed down yesterday. Found three saddle horses tied on the rim but never located the hunters. Descended one on each end of a rimrock. From a little sharp hogback at my end of the rim I jumped a fine buck. He was lying under a fir. Though only 50 yards away he had only one jump to make before he was out of sight. I saw him again as he ran around the other end of the rim, where Howard caught a glimpse of him but did not get a shot. No sooner had the buck disappeared when five does, jumped by Howard, came on his back track and trotted past me at thirty yards—a nearly sure bow shot.

Crossed the creek and topped out on a flat ridge on the east side. Here was a heavy crop of juniper berries and any amount of deer tracks. We saw three bunches of does around this locality but no bucks. Hunted back down another ridge and climbed out again for camp. One must leave Canyon Creek at 3:30 to reach camp by dark. Found a fine pair of shed whitetail horns, four points each side, lying within a few feet of each other. It is seldom they shed simultaneously. There was no bush or limb on which they could have been rubbed off.

13 November

Sunday, so we piously shaved, cut up wood, set sourdough biscuits, sharpened arrows, and similar knickknacks. A beautiful clear day with a roaring wind. This afternoon we are going to rimrock some bucks.

P.M.: Hunted southeasterly toward Canyon Creek. Met a hunter from Oklahoma. He flushed a deer into a little canyon heading out into the prairie and I tried to drive him to Howard but no luck, as he had evidently topped out over the prairie and dropped into the Gila box. Where the Gila box joins the Canyon Creek box we found a long knife-like ridge flanked by palisades. It looks promising. We made one drive at the north end of this ridge which put two whitetail does past Howard. Returned via the Gila rim. Walking along this high prairie in the somber sunset with a howling wind tossing the old cedars along the rim, and a soaring raven croaking over the abyss below, was a solemn and impressive experience. Jumped three whitetails right out on the prairie but it was too late to see horns. They were very pretty bounding over the sea of yellow grama grass with the wind blowing them along like tufts of thistledown. Felt our way down the rocky dugway to camp.

14 November

Decided to make a more thorough exploration of the hills south of the river. Howard went down the box and thence west through the pine ridges. He jumped two blacktail bucks and had three shots at one of them.

I took Brownie and rode south to the breaks of Clear Creek at the foot of Lily Mountain. Saw a whitetail doe soon after leaving the horse. Dropped to the creek and boiled tea in a pretty sunny spot with any number of squirrels all about. Heard a shot to the south, followed by an enormous flock of turkeys sailing across the canyon to the north slope, where I watched them with the glasses as they topped out. Went down the creek to a small trap where I topped out and hunted back westerly along the rim to the horse, reaching him just after sunset. Saw nearly twenty deer along this rim, including two white-

tail and one large blacktail buck. One large whitetail was looking back at me at 70 yards. He jumped at the flash of the bow.
My arrow stuck in his second jump, so that if he had stood
still I would have hit him fairly in the neck.

I also jumped the turkeys again and counted about forty as
they sailed back to the south side of the canyon. I never saw
such a flock, or such a hunting ground.

15 November

Took Howard to Clear Creek by the 'ride and tie' method.
Boiled tea in the canyon, then walked down to the trap. Found
a whole herd of whitetail does, yearlings, and fawns down to
water and watched them for some time but no bucks. Then
started to top out, Howard taking one hogback and I the next.
I bumped into two very large whitetail bucks immediately
after leaving Howard. One offered a standing rifle shot at 90
yards but brush prevented shooting with the bow.

Just short of the top I suddenly saw a large buck in a pine
thicket about 50 yards up the hill, looking me over. I moved
to avoid a bush, drew to the barb at point blank, and let fly.
The unmistakable thud of the arrow striking flesh told me I
had hit—as nearly as I could tell, in the fore ribs or shoulder.
The buck plunged like a pitching bronco and disappeared over
the hogback straight at Howard. I yelled to Howard, who saw
him coming, clearing the oak thicket at every jump. He disappeared in the dip between the two ridges and did not emerge;
we apparently commanded all possible exits. We waited from
3:30 to 4:00 for hemorrhage and then I went in on his track
to the point where Howard last saw him. The slope was so cut
up with other tracks that absolute tracking was impossible. I
followed a plunging track to the point Howard designated but
there was no sign of blood, and a hurried search failed to re-
veal any deer. It was getting dangerously late so we hurried

back to the horse. Had a tough time getting home in the dark.

When full of hot supper I evolved two hopeful theories: (1) if there had been more than one buck I might have been on the wrong track; (2) if the arrow had not been buried deeply why had it not broken off as the buck hinged through the stiff oak brush, and thus been found?

16 November

Back to Clear Creek to put these pretty theories to the test. I spent all morning at the scene of the shooting, and found there had certainly been at least three bucks, two of which had topped out without being seen by either of us. However, there was no blood and no broken arrow on any track. Reluctantly gave up the search.

On my way to the battleground I flushed the whole flock of

102

40 turkeys. They flew north and, soon after, I heard two shots so I knew I had put them into Howard. When he joined me later I found he had had a long shot but no luck.

In the afternoon we hunted the ridge westerly. Saw no whitetail but I got a 70-yard shot at a nice blacktail with three points each side. Overestimated the distance and shot over him. When he ran, Howard saw another one run but got no shot.

We now heard turkeys ahead. Howard went after them and got up on the whole flock at 60 yards but missed. Meanwhile I could see them from the other side but hesitated to shoot at 75 yards, hoping Howard's shot would drive them closer. Finally risked an arrow at 70 yards but some overhead limbs interfered with trajectory and I hit only a juniper tree. When the whole bunch took wing between us and sailed across the canyon, it seemed as if the whole landscape had suddenly turned into turkeys beating upward through the pines. Never again will either of us see such a sight.

A blue evening in camp due to our misses. Got in late.

17 November

Shaved, laundered, sunned, and recorded our misfortunes, which after all netted us some unforgettable pictures even if no meat. Howard went down on the open flat and practiced with his rifle. Our confidence and ambition are returning with clean underwear and warm sunshine. We have three days left, not counting this afternoon.

P.M.: Walked down the Gila box and climbed west to the second open mesa. This slope is torn up with turkey scratchings and deer sign but we found none. Believe they are hanging out in the pine thickets further back. We worked back to the trail, Howard seeing three does. Got into camp before dark for a change.

18 November

Worked the Clear Creek ridge again. It is getting so dry that it is hopeless to stalk deer without a wind except early in the morning before the litter has dried out. Saw a few does and fawns only. When we arrived at the ridge, a dozen turkeys walked by me, two of them in plain sight, the rest under the rim. I had a 30-yard shot at the two but missed. They did not see me and merely hopped a little when the arrow passed as if it were a falling branch. Had another chance at the bunch at 70 yards but did not shoot, fearing they would fly and lose Howard his chance. When he came up, however, we could not find them. Didn't see any deer going back along the rim—no wind.

19 November

Took a gamble at the hills across Clear Creek on the south side. Howard saw three turkeys which had been flushed somewhere and lit near him, but did not offer a shot and we could not find them later. Worked easterly and found Jackson mesa too flat, with no deer or turkey sign. Worked the breaks of the creek but found very little sign. I then walked up the creek to get the horse while Howard climbed the ridge. He saw nothing. I saw a doe and fawn while waiting for him at the trail. In late.

20 November

Worked southeasterly across the ridges with great care. Howard jumped a fine buck out of a pine thicket on a point but he was out of sight in two jumps. When we got to the ridge I made a new search for the buck I hit on the 15th. Once thought I had a lead when I heard some flies buzzing on the ridge north of where he was shot, but I soon found there were

104

flies working on all the ridges. At sunset worked the rim again
but the wind went down on us and there was little chance. Saw
only one doe. The turkeys had been on this rim during the day
and torn it all up.

Found Tipton in camp ready to pack us out.

PRUDENT PROVERBS

1. A Douglas Fir on a hogback under a rimrock is a buck
bed. So is a pine thicket on a point.
2. A piñon thicket is a place for does.
3. When the piñon crop is high-graded, juniper berries are
in order for blacktail. Some whitetail stay in the oaks re-
gardless of nuts.
4. When the edge of a mesa is studded with malpais, it is
prairie and will produce pine only on slopes.
5. Bucks do not necessarily bed on the same side of a
canyon they feed on.
6. Only does water before dark, but both bucks and does
feed before dark.
7. When you stop to blow or look, stop in a shade.
8. Deer cannot be stalked in dry country except in a heavy
wind or early morning. North slopes stay quiet longest.
9. A startled deer will tend to go (1) uphill, (2) into the
wind, (3) around a point, (4) toward cover or rough
ground. When he is startled by sight, no. 2 is the strongest
tendency; when by scent any of the others may be.
10. A turkey cannot smell enough to make scent a factor in
hunting.

Gus's Last Hunt

A.L., E.B.L., E.L.

The Leopold Shack, Baraboo, Wis.

We came up to get us a deer. Took the boat up to Anchor's island, hoping to find it free of hunters. I stood at the lower crossing while Estella and Gus went up the north shore to make a drive. They had no sooner left than I found the fresh track of a deer, crossing the channel from the mainland, and dragging a leg. There was blood. It was clear that somebody's cripple was on the island.

In a few minutes a disgusted-looking hunter appeared. He had followed his cripple to the island but couldn't find her.

While I was talking to the hunter, I heard Gus's 'big-game' yelp. I knew he had found the cripple, and hurried to join him.

When I got there, I found Estella in tears and Gus in the middle of the river. The deer had taken to the water and crossed to the north shore. Gus had followed. On a bar in the middle he had come upon the doe and gotten kicked. I had heard the doe give a loud blat, like a half-grown calf in desperation.

Gus is a weak swimmer because of his crooked leg. I doubted whether he would make the far shore, toward which

106

the current carried him. We hurried back toward the boat, but it was too far to enable me to reach him in time. We were overjoyed when he at last reached the north bank.

It took me half an hour to get to the boat and cross the river. When I reached him he had his hind legs in the water, his forelegs clinging to a sod. He was baying weakly, but was unable to lift his head. I carried him up the bank, but he couldn't stand. His hind quarters were paralyzed, by either exhaustion or the kick from the deer, or both.

Gus recognized me when I carried him up the bank, but he was soon seized by convulsions. I covered him with my coat, but could do nothing else for him. I had to tell him goodbye, and put him out of his misery.

Blue River

I reined up, not sure whether the old cow was dead, or just dying. She had come down out of the drouth-stricken hills to drink, I guess. And now she lay there, quite still, on the hot sandbar. A swarm of brilliant green flies buzzed about her head, and plagued her mouth and eyes. She had craned her neck— the mark was there in the sand—as if for one last look up into the cruel cliffs of Blue River.

I was reflecting on this—especially the ghoulish flies—when it happened. A flash of vermilion—a soft bubbling warble—and a little red bird hovered over the old cow's head, snapping up flies right and left, one after another, for each a cry of ecstasy, in very joy of living. And then with one quick crimson sweep of wing, it disappeared into the green depths of a cottonwood.

Did the old cow see the bird? No. Her dead eyes stared up into the cliffs. Her calf was somewhere up there.

For a while I looked at the old cow, and thought about the little red bird. Then I rode on down Blue River.

The Gila, 1929

A.L., C.S.L., A.S.L.

P. O. Magdalena, N. M.

Armaments

STARKER: 50# yew bow, started by George Kemmerer, finished by Starker, with six footed Alaska Cedar broadheads made by him, and 18 birch broadheads left over from my 1927 Gila trip. Harness and Rawhide quiver of his own make.
CARL: .30–.30 Winchester Carbine.
ALDO: 60# Osage bow; 20 unfooted Alaska Cedar arrows with Weniger broadhead points. Harness and quiver same as 1927.

Going In

6 November, left Albuquerque 8 a.m. Arrived Magdalena 12:30 p.m. Arrived Evans Ranch 4:30 p.m. 7 November, left 8 a.m. with four light packs, arrived Whiterock tank in a rain 2 p.m. Saw one buck antelope, single, in Evans' pasture, and two herds of 22 and about 6 on Burnt Corral mesa. Sent packs back but kept 'Tango,' a black pony with a white star on his forehead and an artistic temperament. Heavy wind till bedtime (8 p.m.). Carl slept cold and I hard.

110

8 November

A bright fine morning. Up in dark at 4 a.m. and when sun came out started dolling up camp. We are under a big spreading alligator juniper on the edge of a pretty park full of fine grama grass. It is 200 yards down to Evans' stock tank for water. There is enough oak and juniper wood within 200 yards of camp to furnish the U. S. Army, only they wouldn't appreciate its fine qualities.

In the afternoon we de-horned a big dead juniper only 50 yards from camp and piled up half a cord of fragrant wood—also brought in some oak. Also started the sourdough and other similar ceremonies, including a pot of beans. Dined on beans and cornbread in a fall of snow which started in the middle of the afternoon and by bedtime was two inches deep. This will make fine prospecting for deer tomorrow. Had music in our snug dry camp after dinner while all the rest of the world outside was white and cold.

9 November

Up before daylight and breakfasted mightily on sourdough hotcakes. Off about 8 a.m. just as a fog was lifting on the white world. On the mesa prairie just northwest of camp, came on the tracks of a big bunch of deer, including at least one large buck, which had drifted west during the night—possibly moving out of the East Gila country because of the hunters congregated there. We back-tracked them to where they had topped out of the Whiterock Rincon and decided this would be a dandy pass on opening day.

Carl and Starker then prospected the rolling hills to the northwest where they saw three bunches of does totaling 13 (with only one fawn and no bucks). They also shot a cottontail but lost him.

I headed northeast along the Montoya drift fence and where it crosses the first little canyon jumped two bucks, one very large (at least 8 and possibly 10 points) and one smaller. They bounded north over the prairie to Windfall Canyon. The big one offered me a broadside standing rifle shot before he ran at 125 yards. At the same time two other deer stood watching me on the hill to the east. I never found out what they were.

We met at camp for lunch and then explored southward, locating a pass that would be good but for a drift fence. From the pasture hill back of camp we saw 30 antelope feeding on the mesa to the south. The whole immensity of the Gila basin lay spread before us in a sunset so quiet you could hear a cricket chirp. It was a sight worth the whole trip.

Had a prize dinner of ham, hominy, and sourdough biscuits we had set at noon. Spent the evening planning tomorrow's campaign.

My candle is dripping and the boys are in bed, so no more today.

10 November—Opening Day

Starker and I stayed in the 'pass' just north of camp while Carl went farther on to Windfall Canyon, where I saw the two bucks go yesterday. Nothing came our way on the pass except a doe and a coyote, both routed by the opening bombardment. We got plenty cold, however. After boiling some erbswurst we started to drive the little short canyons coming off the rim into Montoya Canyon. The first three yielded nothing, but just as I was approaching the fourth (now called Buck Canyon), a big buck jumped out and headed down the draw instead of up toward where Starker was stationed. He had not gone more than 200 yards out of sight when I heard the crack of a rifle— one shot only. I was just starting to tell myself that I had presented some stranger with a nice buck when 'toot-toot-toot'

came three blasts of our little horn, the agreed-upon signal for
'dead deer—come and help.'

Straker and I both heard it and ran up with a loud whoop
to meet Carl emerging from the little draw with the hoped-for
grin on his face.

Buck Day on the Gila (C.S.L.)

We were late out of camp and the sun was up when I left Aldo
and Starker on the pass above the Whiterock. It is about a
mile across the mesa to Windfall Canyon, where Aldo had seen
two bucks the day before. I followed the old Montoya drift
fence and was still 200 yards from the canyon rim when five
bucks went over the horizon just east of me, and ran parallel
with my course. They were looking back and had not seen
me.

It took them a long time to disappear into the canyon and
I sneaked to the rim about 200 yards above where they had
entered. In a few minutes they all moved out on to an open
point just across from me and not more than 200 yards from
me. I watched them for fully half an hour. They were sus-
picious but not frightened—four big bucks and one spiker.
Finally they moved back into the canyon bottom below me but
out of sight, so I slipped a few yards closer and waited for an
opening.

They slowly froze me out and I decided to try a shot. One
of the big ones stepped across an opening and I let go at his
shoulder—a miss. The place was suddenly alive with bounding
bucks. Two went up the canyon and three took right out into
the open again across from me. They stopped on the opposite
ridge and looked around for several minutes, then disappeared
into a small draw, but still were not badly scared.

I cut down into Windfall and went up about ⅜ of a mile,
then climbed over the open ridge into the head of their draw

and worked down it very slowly. There was practically no wind. From bush to tree and tree to rock, always using my glasses, I worked down slowly. At last there he was, right in the middle of my glass, a fine big buck, about 125 yards away,

right in the bottom of the draw and headed my way. Two smaller bucks were behind him. I was kneeling on a flat rock behind a low bush, so settled down to watch and wait. That buck took 30 minutes to move as many feet and was on the lookout 90 per cent of the time. My knees got stiffer and my neck likewise but I was determined to stick it out and get a

114

real shot with no alibis. Finally they practically stopped moving and I decided the time had come.

As I raised the old .30, I realized too late that the buck was head-on instead of broadside but he was looking right at me and it was too late to retreat. I aimed low and carefully but missed clean. Away they went, again across the open hillside.

The chest of a ten-point blacktail is a ten-inch circle. How can a man miss it at 90 yards? Things looked a bit blue from a meat point of view but I was sure having a whale of a time. No blood sign on the trail of the fugitives. I worked down the draw to the canyon and then down the bottom of the canyon. A pipe and a little lunch in a warm sunny spot while seven does passed up the opposite side.

Jumped two bucks right after lunch—they were plenty close but saw me first—no more running shots for me. Worked down about half a mile and then climbed out on the south side and worked the mesa rim back toward the Whiterock. Three does stampeded out of a waterhole. Farther on another good buck jumped close by, but kept so well to cover I had no chance.

Got back to the east fork of the Montoya Box, where we were to have met for lunch, and decided to rest a while and watch. Picked an opening where I could see across the draw and sat down beside a small juniper bush. It began to look like the end of a buckless day and I wondered where the boys were and what their luck had been. A stone rattled on the opposite hillside and there he was, coming on the sneak, a big one and straight toward me. I shifted to one knee and picked out the opening where I hoped he might pass, and he did, at a walking trot. No time for fancy aiming but he was close, about 70 yards.

It was a lucky shot, as he dropped in his tracks and never

moved. I covered him for a few seconds and then gave the old horn three long blasts. And then came the real surprise and treat. Aldo and Starker answered the horn by voice and soon appeared on the buck's back-track. They had jumped him themselves and driven him right into my ambush. It was a lucky break for me and we had a great celebration together while we hung him up and took pictures. Eleven points and in good condition. The liver and heart went back to camp with us for dinner.

11 November

All three of us started with 'Tango' to pack in Carl's buck. On the way I could see a glimpse of half a dozen deer we jumped just under the Whiterock only half a mile from camp. We found the buck as we left him and hardly frozen. Took some pictures and also the following weights (part of them obtained later but presented here to give his complete specifications).

Weight

Entrails	36	pounds
Liver and kidneys, est.	8	"
Blood, est.	5	"
Total drawings	49	"
Head and hide	20	"
Waste, est.	6	"
Total non-meat	75	"
Meat, including feet and neck	100	"
Total weight, live	175	pounds

116

THE GILA, 1929

Measurements

Horns:

Widest spread, tip to tip . . . . 27"
Girth at base, steel tape over warts. . 4½"
Total points 11
Ears, tip to tip . . . . 22"
Length track:
Front . . . . 2¼"
Hind . . . . 2"

Carl took the buck into camp while Starker and I went over to Windfall Canyon across the prairie. Carl went to the mouth of Windfall and drove toward us on horseback. He sent two yearlings past me at about 20 yards. Later some other party drove several bucks past us—too far for a shot. We skipped over the prairie to Buck Canyon, where Carl next tried to drive them back but no luck except some does. Carl then rode to camp while Starker and I headed for a high juniper hill to the west. I went in one side and he on the other. A whole procession of does and four big bucks strung past me at about 60 yards but the brush was too thick to shoot. Starker tried one shot but fell short. The whole bunch then showed us their heels as they disappeared over the next ridge to the west.

On the way back to camp we saw some does. Had kidney stew from the buck.

12 November

Carl stayed in camp to skin and butcher his buck. Starker and I went back to where we saw the four bucks yesterday. On the way I drove a piñon point for Starker and at the head of the draw saw a deer bedded down under a piñon, looking at me not fifty yards off. He was directly into the sun and I could hardly find him with the glass, much less tell whether he had

117

horns. Finally I thought I could see spikes but didn't want to shoot as I would have had to shoot him straight in the face, and besides there was a limb in the way. So I decided to risk walking straight on in the hope of finding a line for a broad-

side shot. The deer then jumped up and imagine my surprise to see an eight-point whitetail! Of course he kept in the brush. I tried one arrow, but without effect, except that the arrow buried half an inch deep in a porous malpais rock.

In the draw where we saw the four bucks yesterday we found nothing but some does.

118

We then went west to the next slope to hunt it back to camp. Just before we got there we heard a shot in the canyon to the north. We ducked for a juniper and waited five minutes, but saw nothing, so went on to a kind of saddle. Then a big buck (about six or eight points) came down out of the north and passed right by the juniper where we had been! I tried an arrow but it was too far. The arrow splintered.

Starker then started down the slope, the crest of which I was to follow on the way home. Hardly had he gone when a four-point buck preceded by a doe came out of the canyon to the north and entered our canyon on Starker's tracks. There had been another shot so I was hoping he would be looking back and would see these deer. They were a long shot for me, as I had moved off 75 yards down the ridge. Soon there was another shot, followed by another four-pointer. Then another, followed by still another four-pointer with a broken foreleg. This one I should have tried to intercept, but still hoping that Starker was there, I did not. Finally two hunters came along— seemingly unaware of all the game they had put up, and I was sure they would stampede all three bucks right by me. Nothing came. Then I blew my horn, and getting no answer, knew that Starker had not been there at all, but had proceeded down the slope as per his instructions! Thus did I miss four chances at bucks in 30 minutes.

We got into camp at 2:30 and found Carl had the buck all butchered. We shaved and roasted the ribs over oak coals. They looked fine but were tough—too early to be good yet. However, sourdough bread and macaroni consoled us.

13 November

Starker and I went back to the saddle west of juniper hill while Carl rode to Black Mountain to look for turkey. We found everything full of hunters and did not get any shots or good hunts. I found a spikehorn which had been shot in his bed and not claimed, probably because his horns were a little short of the legal 6-inch limit. It was very cold standing on pass.

14 November

All of us went south along the rim to the TJ points. We could see deer below us under the rim and one outfit we passed was bombarding a buck half a mile away across the canyon. Went down the TJ trail and on the first hill we drove, Carl jumped a very large blacktail buck who eluded two attempts to drive him and finally left the country. In the dry box canyon north of TJ points we found much turkey sign. Drove this canyon north and got separated. I found a good deer country on the east ridge of this canyon but could not work it alone. Finally located Starker and climbed out the little box below camp, the head of which is full of rich vegetation and has several pools of water. Found Carl had hunted north to the head of the canyon and was in camp. This was a stiff but interesting day.

15 November

General laundry and housecleaning till 10 a.m. Then climbed down the Pothole Box into the big canyon, where Carl hunted turkey while Starker and I tried the deer. On the way down the slope, Carl jumped a big buck—possibly the same one we hunted on the TJ hill yesterday. He went diagonally across the canyon. Soon after, a tremendous bombardment started on the TJ hill. We got into position and soon a doe came panting up and first nearly ran me down and then Starker. The big buck came back just behind her, but the doe having scented me and seen Starker, the buck was able to split exactly the distance between us and remain out of range of both.

We had intended to work the mesa west of this canyon in the afternoon but we heard other hunters up there. After cooking lunch with Carl we drove south toward the TJ points. Jumped several deer but there was not enough wind—they seemed to know both our locations and to make their getaway accordingly. Just at sunset Starker saw a big buck in the rincon below the TJ hill. He wanted to follow him up toward the rimrock, but I was done up and couldn't. Climbed out the TJ trail, getting into camp late.

16 November

Spent the morning making jerky and cleaning up around camp. Used one whole ham and one shoulder of Carl's buck. We find it dries nearly completely in one day when turned over, and ought to be 'done' in two days. It shrinks 75 per cent in area as well as thickness. In the afternoon we made a little hunt on the Whiterock hill. In spite of the fact that the hill had been bombarded this morning, Carl, who was doing the driving, jumped three bucks. One of them was drifting in past the corral in the head of Montoya Canyon. Carl had two open shots at 80 yards and the arrow went just over the deer's back both times. Tomorrow we will concentrate on this hill.

17 November

Again worked the home hill but it was very quiet. Saw one buck on the Whiterock but he offered no shot. In evening made another hunt toward the Montoya box, where I had a fall off a pine log. Saw some does and yearlings near the mouth of Buck Canyon but saw no bucks. A beautiful quiet evening.

18 November

Carl drove the malpais box at the waterhole crossing and put a beautiful buck across the rock face just above it. He had a 70-yard shot nearly straight down off the rimrock and missed him by only a few inches.

The three of us then made a careful work of the juniper canyon ridge. A fair west breeze had sprung up and we got close to a number of deer. One passed me at 60 yards but in shadow and behind brush. I never made out whether it was a buck or a doe.

At evening we arrived at the point of the ridge. Three bucks which some other hunters had stirred got up a long way ahead of me and circled to the right. I then took a stand at what I knew was the crossing at the point of the ridge on which Carl and Starker were working abreast. Soon I heard deer, and made out three small deer coming down the hill diagonally past me, but obscured by brush. When directly opposite me, and about 60 yards distant, they stopped, seemed to ponder the fate of nations, and then to my utter surprise, plunged squarely down the hill and directly at me, but still obscured by brush. As they filed across a very small opening I made out that the first two were does, while the last seemed to be a spiker. I drew on a clear opening under a juniper where I knew they would pass, about 30 yards to my left, and in a moment the two does filed by in that peculiar hesitating trot which makes it uncertain whether the next instant will bring a total stop or a terrified leap. Then came the spiker. I was not yet sure whether his horns were 6 inches (the legal minimum) and devoted the first instant of clear vision to verifying this fact, instead of to a final appraisal of distance and aim, as I should have. Then I shot. The arrow passed over his back and splintered harmlessly on the rocks. I had held only two feet under instead of three feet.

The spiker bounded up the hill. At 120 yards I shot a second arrow, just as a sort of goodbye.

More perfect chances to make a kill do not occur, except in deer hunters' dreams.

A little later Starker came down the hill, looking sheepish. I

122

assumed he was ashamed of my performance, but soon learned that he had missed a similar shot at the same spiker. It was his arrow that had pushed them down to my stand.

19 November

A clear, still, windless day, worthless for hunting. We tried the Juniper Hill country again. Carl and Starker saw a very large buck but could not contrive anything more than a rifle chance. On the way home we drove a point near camp where we had located a buck in the morning and thought the rimrocks would force him to pass the Whiterock Tank. He knew the topography better than we. He cut back below us on the very edge of the lower rim.

20 November

Packed out to Evans Ranch.

MAXIMS OF AN UNSUCCESSFUL DEER HUNTER

1. A deer never follows anything. If he can cross a ridge, a rimrock, a ravine, or even a prairie, he will do so, especially if it is into the wind.
2. The doe always comes first—the buck after.
3. A whitetail will be in his bed and let you pass.
4. A deer will not jump from scent except close by, but he will sneak out as far as the scent will carry.
5. In a drive, it's the first run that counts. A drive is no good unless it proceeds slowly enough for each man to sit down half the time.
6. The opposite hillside is always less brushy than the side you are on. It is the best place to shoot.
7. The spikers that run with does and yearlings are an easier chance for bow and arrow than the big bucks.

123

8. One windy day is worth a week of calm weather, and a windy evening is best of all.
9. Hunting abreast, into or across the wind, and not over two bowshots apart, is the best formation. Three abreast is better than two. Driving to a stationary man on a 'stand' seldom works.
10. Clean your glasses daily, and never hunt without them. Good illumination and clean lenses are necessary to discern horns in shadow, and are much more important than high magnification. Examine every 'doe' twice.
11. Don't be too cautious. You can run up on a trotting or jumping deer, where you couldn't move a foot on a standing or sneaking deer without detection.
12. If in doubt whether to shoot, do so at once, provided only the deer be broadside.
13. Keep a practice arrow (marked for the purpose with a section of rubber tube on the nock) and shoot a few shots daily in the least stony spot you can find.

USE AND CARE OF VENISON AS LEARNED AT WHITEROCK DEER CAMP

The liver can be braised the first day but should not be broiled until the second. It is the best part of the deer.

The ribs are tough and strong as late as the third day and possibly do not become good until much later.

Roasts and chops may be braised by the fifth day but should not be broiled or fried before the seventh.

All meat cures more quickly after skinning.

Jerky may be started five days after skinning. It dries perfectly in two days if cut thin and turned after one day. It shrinks 75 per cent in area and probably more than that in weight (note: find out the shrinkage in weight on next trip).

Jerky should be cut along the grain while the meat is partly frozen. Slices down to ¼-inch thickness are entirely feasible. The shoulders and hams are best for jerky. Remove all fat.

The hide should be stretched on the ground with sharp wooden pegs, Indian style.

A can of tomato greatly improves venison broth that tends to be 'strong' because of insufficient curing.

Baste all broilings with bacon fat applied with a pine-needle brush.

A buck with one inch of fat on the rump is moderately fat; a buck with less is thin; two inches of fat is found only in piñon-nut or juniper-berry years.

Kidneys are very choice but because of the suet should be braised, not boiled. The heart and neck are good as soup stock and boiled meat.

The Deer Swath

One hot afternoon in August I sat under the elm, idling, when I saw a deer pass across a small opening a quarter mile east. A deer trail crosses our farm, and at this point any deer traveling is briefly visible from the shack.

I then realized that half an hour before I had moved my chair to the best spot for watching the deer trail; that I had done this habitually for years, without being clearly conscious of it. This led to the thought that by cutting some brush I could widen the zone of visibility. Before night the swath was cleared, and within the mouth I detected several deer which otherwise could likely have passed unseen.

The new deer swath was pointed out to a series of week-end guests for the purpose of watching their later reactions to it. It was soon clear that most of them forgot it quickly, while others watched it, as I did, whenever chance allowed. The upshot was the realization that there are four categories of outdoors men: deer hunters, duck hunters, bird hunters, and non-hunters. These categories have nothing to do with sex or age, or accoutrements; they represent four diverse habits of the human eye. The deer hunter habitually watches the next bend; the duck hunter watches the skyline; the bird hunter watches the dog; the non-hunter does not watch.

THE DEER SWATH

When the deer hunter sits down he sits where he can see ahead, and with his back to something. The duck hunter sits where he can see overhead, and behind something. The nonhunter sits where he is comfortable. None of these watches the dog. The bird hunter watches only the dog, and always knows where the dog is, whether or not visible at the moment. The dog's nose is the bird hunter's eye. Many hunters who carry a shotgun in season have never learned to watch the dog, or to interpret his reactions to scent.

There are good outdoors men who do not conform to these categories. There is the ornithologist who hunts by ear, and uses the eye only to follow up on what his ear has detected. There is the botanist who hunts by eye, but at much closer range; he is a marvel at finding plants, but seldom sees birds or mammals. There is the forester who sees only trees, and the insects and fungi that prey upon trees; he is oblivious to all else. And finally there is the sportsman who sees only game, and regards all else as of little interest or value.

There is one illusive mode of hunting which I cannot associate exclusively with any of these groups: the search for scats, tracks, feathers, dens, roostings, rubbings, dustings, diggings, feedings, fightings, or preyings collectively known to woodsmen as 'reading sign.' This skill is rare, and too often seems to be inverse to book learning.

The counterpart of reading animal sign exists in the plant field, but skill is equally rare in occurrence, and illusive in distribution. To prove this I cite the African explorer who detected the scratchings of a lion on the bark of a tree, 20 feet up. The scratchings, he said, had been made when the tree was young.

That biological jack-of-all-trades called ecologist tries to be and do all of these things. Needless to say, he does not succeed;

127

the best he can do is to alternate his modes of hunting. I find that while hunting plants, I can give only indifferent attention to animals, and vice versa. The ecologist has the choice of setting forth with glass, gun, axe, trowel, or shovel, and adjusting his eye and mind to the tools at hand.

The common denominator of all hunters is the realization that there is always something to hunt. The world teems with creatures, processes, and events that are trying to elude you; there is always a deer, and always a swath down which he can be seen. Every ground is a hunting ground, whether it lies between you and the curbstone, or in those illimitable woods where rolls the Oregon. The final test of the hunter is whether he is keen to go hunting in a vacant lot.

Deadening

The old oak had been girdled and was dead.

There are degrees of death in abandoned farms. Some old houses cock an eye at you as if to say 'Somebody will move in. Wait and see.'

But this farm was different. Girdling the old oak to squeeze one last crop out of the barnyard has the same finality as burning the furniture to keep warm.

Sierra Madre, 1937

A.L., C.S.L., A.S.L.

P. O. Colonia Pacheco,
Chihuahua, Mexico

23 December

Finally arrived at Colonia Pacheco after surviving the hazards of two days of Mexican travel. The Chihuahua Flyer landed us safely in Casas Grandes yesterday afternoon but Mr. Cluff didn't get in with his truck until dark, owing to snow and bad roads. Spent a cold night in the Hotel Regis, but we were all impressed with the luxury of running water. The proprietress, after showing us our rooms, ushered us pompously down the hall to the door labeled 'Caballeros,' and pointed with pride to the Crane fixtures that really flushed, obviously an innovation in Casas Grandes. The Cine which we took in during the evening was probably our coldest hour to date; the hall would serve admirably as an ice box. The melodrama was quite unintelligible to us gringos, but was apparently a source of considerable enjoyment to the natives, judging by the reactions of the house.

The truck ride out this morning was an adventure by itself.

The road follows an old logging railroad grade up the mountain, and in one cut a ten-ton boulder had slipped during the night, apparently blocking the road. The measured opening proved to be about three inches narrower than the truck box. Nevertheless, by a series of carefully manipulated plunges, we got it through, how we still don't clearly understand. That International truck with its mountain training must have quarterback hips.

24 December

Starker took Clarence's old shotgun down to the creek this morning and bagged a little meat for camp—three snipe and a teal. There were at least a dozen snipe, and some 30 or 40 ducks, mostly teal and mallards.

The pack train set out at 10:00 a.m. and pulled into camp in mid-afternoon. We had plenty of time to get things organized before dark. Clarence and Harl turned right home so as not to miss the Christmas dance.

Carl took a walk before dark and put up two does but failed to get a shot.

25 December (A.S.L.)

Christmas day! We all forgot to even exchange greetings until sometime after breakfast.

Worked the hills around Lookout Point all day but saw only seven does and one little spiker. Carl took two long running shots in the hope of knocking down some camp meat, but made no hits. I took a flyer at a jumping doe (50 yards) but the only result was a shattered arrow.

Just before evening Dad and Carl walked the little mesa across the creek from camp and jumped two big bucks. Both sneaked out wild, however.

I took the shotgun and walked up the hill back of camp

after Mearns quail. Found only two but nailed them both. I am going to carry a slingshot on the horse after this and try and take some specimen skins.

A cup of cherry bounce and a good plate of beans were ample Christmas celebration.

26 December

We have meat in camp tonight. Carl knocked down a nice little doe with a clean shoulder shot. Four does crossed the point 30 yards behind him, and he took the smallest one. A

big buck was following them 20 seconds behind but Carl didn't see him till too late.

We saw 4 bucks and 11 does during the day's hunt on Diablo Mesa. The bucks all seem to be on points where they can duck out of sight in a split second. Jump shooting is apparently no dice with a bow.

Just as we were reconvening at the horses, Carl and I spotted a bunch of gobblers on the slope of Perdita Mesa a mile to the northeast. We shall give them a chase tomorrow.

Mr. Johnson (Harl's son) was waiting for us at the horses. He saw a javelena not 20 minutes before we came.

Liver and kidney stew for dinner and early to bed.

27 December

Floyd took us over the Perdita Mesa and back down Turkey Ridge. Saw one buck near the Chocolate Drop but few other deer. Much turkey sign on the hogback leading up to Perdita from the west and also a good deal of deer sign on the north rim of the mesa bordering Smoke Canyon. No shots with either bow or gun.

28 December

Explored the Crack Canyon region for the first time. Saw a large number of deer and the country looks very workable. No turkey sign.

29 December

Back to Crack Canyon with even more deer today. Carl knocked down a yearling for camp meat, but after a minute's struggle she regained her feet and escaped, even under fire. She was probably just creased on the shoulder, as it was a head-on shot and Carl has been shooting high. Very little blood shed, and her track was impossible to follow in the rocks. We hope she will be none the worse for her shock.

Put a fine buck out of the Short Canyon but he topped out the head just before Carl got there.

30 December

This was buck day! After a hard day's work, we were taking a last swing around the point at the mouth of Long Canyon and I put out two fine bucks bedded together on the point. They topped over from me and skirted down the low shoulder running north from the point, and ran right into Carl. The ensuing bombardment dropped one in his tracks with a broken back, a fine eight-pointer weighing 80 pounds dressed. We were all surprised at the small size. It was a happy party that rode into camp tonight. He will be properly hung up in the morning to decorate the camp.

31 December (A.S.L.)

This was Carl's birthday and Dad came up with an appropriate 'cake' for the occasion, a cookie with a little dickey bird on it and one candle. A round of cherry bounce marked the general celebration, and then to bed.

Carl started on a quest for turkeys, riding the Bear Canyon area with Clarence. Found no sign.

Dad and I had an easy day in the same general neighborhood, with plenty of time off for a nap after lunch and some bow practice on the bottom of a little dried-up lake. An archer should find some place to shoot every day. It takes little time, and keeps you in some sort of shape when that one chance does come along. You soon get stiff and off form if you don't shoot at all.

Speaking of getting stiff, the beds are getting harder and more compact every night. The rim of my hip-hole feels like that rock ledge around the Perdita.

1 January

New Year's Day was passed just like any other day, save that Carl killed another buck. We were riding the Perdita neighborhood for turkey and happened to spot a doe and fawn ahead down in the Perdita itself. We dismounted and slipped up on them and up jumped a fine little buck hitherto unseen. Carl

134

took him standing at 200 yards and put him down, but he was only paunched and took some more killing before he dropped for good. He weighed only 60 pounds dressed, and had a tiny little head of eight points that would near fit in your hat.

Floyd is warming up some during the evening song fests, and seems to know an infinite number of new Spanish songs. We are all now working on 'Concha Querida.'

2 January (A.S.L.)

Carl is still looking for turkeys, and finding much sign but no birds. His edict is that 'Turkeys is where you find 'em,' which is probably pretty sound philosophy.

Dad and I loafed on top of Perdita Mesa. An old doe and her two yearlings walked right into us on the open mesa top and I had a standing shot at the doe at 45 yards. The arrow seemed to brush right over her withers, and she herded her youngsters right out of there in a hurry. It was an easy shot that I shouldn't have missed. We weren't very sorry, however, but would have liked a crack at one of those yearlings.

Since that one rainy day we have been having beautiful mild weather. It would be better for hunting, however, if there were more wind—still, dry days are noisy.

3 January (A.S.L.)

Today we pulled stakes at the Bathtub Camp and moved down onto the river at the foot of Chocolate Drop Hill. This is a beautiful camp site with many oaks for scenery and good wood. We have picked out the limb where game will be hung from now on.

It was so warm when we finished setting up camp that Carl and I decided to try a swim in the river. This we did, and hereby take occasion to recommend the Gavilan as good drinking water but poor swimming—we were paralyzed for an hour.

We are all reinspired by getting into a new camp with new country to explore. Tomorrow we shall have a look at the Breaks of the Blue high on the rim above us.

While taking an evening walk below camp I saw an otter. From a little cliff above the stream I watched him slide across a deep, still pool far below and then shoot a rapids to disappear around the bend. Clarence says in all the years he has lived here he has never had a look at one, though he often finds tracks.

There are fresh tracks of wolf on the trail down the river. We wish they would give us a concert some evening.

4 January (A.S.L.)

Dad and I got out at daylight and hunted the Chocolate Drop back of camp. Saw two bunches of deer, and I got a flash shot at a little fawn in the oak scrub but failed to catch up with him. We crossed over to the West Rim for the rest of the day and found a number of deer in the breaks of the Blue Ridge. I had one brush shot at a standing doe but overshot by a foot. She was 50 instead of 60 yards. Our drives failed to work, the bucks in particular preferring to run downhill.

Carl rode all day alone after turkey. He found the Smoke Ridge bunch in the saddle at the east end of the mesa and put out three hens at 30 yards after skirting around them on foot. But he was carrying a rifle! Turkey hunters will carry shotguns from now on.

The glee club enjoyed an evening workout.

5 January (A.S.L.)

The bows went back into the Breaks of the Blue while Carl and Floyd rode into the Upper Diablo country after the bunch

136

of gobblers. Dad had an 80-yard shot at a doe in her bed and laid the arrow in the rocks at her feet. An archer tends to undershoot the long shots and overshoot the close ones.

Carl put up four of the bunch and dropped one big gobbler on a reflush. He fell with both wings broken into a manzanita thicket and made his escape, apparently down a narrow draw. An hour and a half of combing the thicket on hands and knees failed to yield a trace of him, save the hatful of feathers where he fell. Page Flick!

A good bird dog that knew how to heel would be a tremendous advantage in working turkeys. The scattered singles will often run a hundred yards before laying. Cripples like Carl's would be in the hand with a dog. He would also be handy for working Mearns quail.

Floyd killed a fine eight-point buck and also a fawn for camp meat in the foothills of Smoke Mesa.

6 January (A.S.L.)

I turned into a turkey hunter and rode all day with Carl up through the Diablo country and back by way of Smoke Mesa. Much fresh sign but no birds. Saw only one deer on the whole ride, whereas Carl and Floyd had seen 20 on the same route the day before.

The little coves and hills around camp failed to yield a bow shot for Dad, though he saw a fair number of deer, including several bucks.

Clarence rode up into the Blue in search of a pair of spurs. He failed to find the spurs but killed a big buck and saw several turkeys. Also found the carcass of a big colt that was clearly a fresh lion kill. It was covered with grass and limbs in good lion style. No traps in camp.

7 January (A.S.L.)

All three of us worked the Smoke and Perdita Mesas for deer and turkey. After a long day's search we finally jumped the Perdita bunch on the west rim. Carl spotted down 4 birds near the little saddle in the west hogback and we pushed our power hard to reach them before they ran. Jumped one old hen and she got away by virtue of some very clever maneuvering behind

138

a pine downfall and some gun trouble on my part. We worked that Johnnie-jump-up till dark but failed to locate the other three. It later appeared they had run.

The evening in camp was spent plotting against that scattered bunch, with Clarence designated to play the lead role as head-caller with a stick of macaroni. All rolled in early.

8 January (A.S.L.)

It was very dark indeed when Clarence, Carl, and I pointed toward Perdita Mesa after a scanty breakfast of cold venison and java. We arrived at the saddle somewhat scratched and disheveled after a brushy ride in the dark, but with plenty of time to get into position before dawn broke. Just as the horned owl gave his last call and it became possible to distinguish objects on the opposite hillside, Clarence started his chirping on that macaroni. He was immediately rewarded with an answer about 300 yards to the west and beyond the saddle where the birds had scattered the night before. A little conversation ensued, and soon other voices were heard coming closer. In ten minutes the birds appeared on the opposite hilltop, a bunch of six! This was the critical moment and suspense was intense as they stood there with heads raised, looking and trying to decide whether to keep coming. A low, nonchalant chirp or two from the macaroni stick turned the trick, and here they came, single file down the hill on an easy trot. They dropped out of sight into the gully, and reappeared after what seemed an interminable time, 20 yards to Carl's left and 25 yards from me. At Clarence's signal the bombardment started, and when the smoke cleared two birds were down for good. Our shooting was poor, we should have had more, and the big old gobbler in the bunch escaped unscratched, but we were delighted with what we had. Both birds were young, Carl's a-coming gobbler with a little beard, and mine a hen.

On the way back to camp we stopped and Clarence suggested we try another chirp or two to try and locate the scattered singles. We slipped out to a sharp point, and there to our surprise he got immediate answers. Several birds came slowly toward us, but instead of coming straight they cautiously swung in a wide circle and unfortunately ran across our saddled horses. That was the end of those birds; they took immediate flight and we saw them no more. A saddled horse, Clarence says, will frighten a turkey as much as a man.

Spent the rest of the day up in the Breaks of the Blue. I had a 40-yard shot at a spiker, looking at his head and ears over a rise. Shot for his shoulder, and though the arrow skimmed through the grass as it crossed the rise, it passed just over his withers. A definite rule should be, 'Shoot for the head when that's all you can see.'

Dad was nearly run over by the granddad buck of the whole Gavilan. Clarence put him out, and he ran right into Carl who turned him down toward Dad with a well-placed charge of shot in the dirt. He arrived there really making knots and so took Dad by storm that he didn't even shoot. There should be traffic laws to prevent that sort of thing.

9 January (A.S.L.)

Last day in camp and quite a lazy one. Dad took a daylight hunt while the rest of us slept. The rest of the morning was spent putting up a turkey skin, shaving, and getting ready to pack.

Took a last walk with the bows toward late afternoon, but over on the lower Perdita hogback, where yesterday we saw a dozen deer, there were only an old doe and her fawn.

Held the last meeing of the glee club after a supper of turkey legs, quail, and venison cutlets.

140

10 January (A.S.L.)

Broke camp and were on the trail before the sun rose. I rode ahead to Bear Canyon to pick up Dad's belt and miscellany kit, and rejoined the party near Clarence's upper fields.

Mrs. Lunt's enchiladas were a fine lunch for a hungry troupe of riders.

With luggage piled high on Mr. Cluff's International, we waved *adios* to the Sierra Madres for this year. Once more the deer have evaded our arrows, and we took time as we rode along to try and analyze why we had failed and what to do next time. It's a great game.

Part III

THE ROUND RIVER

Conservation

Conservation is a bird that flies faster than the shot we aim at it.

I can remember the day when I was sure that reforming the Game Commission would give us conservation. A group of us worked like Trojans cleaning house at the Capitol. When we got through we found we had just started. We learned that you can't conserve game by itself; to rebuild the game resource you must first rebuild the game range, and this means rebuilding the people who use it, and all of the things they use it for. The job we aspired to perform with a dozen volunteers is now baffling a hundred professionals. The job we thought would take five years will barely be started in fifty.

Our target, then, is a receding one. The task grows greater year by year, but so does its importance. We begin by seeking a few trees or birds; to get them we must build a new relationship between men and land.

Conservation is a state of harmony between men and land. By land is meant all of the things on, over, or in the earth. Harmony with land is like harmony with a friend; you cannot cherish his right hand and chop off his left. That is to say, you cannot love game and hate predators; you cannot conserve the waters and waste the ranges; you cannot build the forest and mine the farm. The land is one organism. Its parts, like our own parts, compete with each other and co-operate with each other. The competitions are as much a part of the inner workings as the co-operations. You can regulate them—cautiously—but not abolish them.

The outstanding scientific discovery of the twentieth century is not television, or radio, but rather the complexity of the land organism. Only those who know the most about it can appreciate how little we know about it. The last word in ignorance is the man who says of an animal or plant: 'What good is it?' If the land mechanism as a whole is good, then every part is good, whether we understand it or not. If the biota, in the course of aeons, has built something we like but do not

146

understand, then who but a fool would discard seemingly useless parts? To keep every cog and wheel is the first precaution of intelligent tinkering.

Have we learned this first principle of conservation: to preserve all the parts of the land mechanism? No, because even the scientist does not yet recognize all of them.

In Germany there is a mountain called the Spessart. Its south slope bears the most magnificent oaks in the world. American cabinetmakers, when they want the last word in quality, use Spessart oak. The north slope, which should be the better, bears an indifferent stand of Scotch pine. Why? Both slopes are part of the same state forest; both have been managed with equally scrupulous care for two centuries. Why the difference?

Kick up the litter under the oaks and you will see that the leaves rot almost as fast as they fall. Under the pines, though, the needles pile up as a thick duff; decay is much slower. Why? Because in the Middle Ages the south slope was preserved as a deer forest by a hunting bishop; the north slope was pastured, plowed, and cut by settlers, just as we do with our woodlots in Wisconsin and Iowa today. Only after this period of abuse was the north slope replanted to pines. During this period of abuse something happened to the microscopic flora and fauna of the soil. The number of species was greatly reduced, i.e. the digestive apparatus of the soil lost some of its parts. Two centuries of conservation have not sufficed to restore these losses. It required the modern microscope, and a century of research in soil science, to discover the existence of these 'small cogs and wheels' which determine harmony or disharmony between men and land in the Spessart.

American conservation is, I fear, still concerned for the most part with show pieces. We have not yet learned to think in terms of small cogs and wheels. Look at our own back yard: at the prairies of Iowa and southern Wisconsin. What is the most valuable part of the prairie? The fat black soil, the chernozem. Who built the chernozem? The black prairie was built by the prairie plants, a hundred distinctive species of grasses, herbs, and shrubs; by the prairie fungi, insects, and bacteria; by the prairie mammals and birds, all interlocked in one humming community of co-operations and competitions, one biota. This biota, through ten thousand years of living and dying, burning and growing, preying and fleeing, freezing and thawing, built that dark and bloody ground we call prairie.

Our grandfathers did not, could not, know the origin of their prairie empire. They killed off the prairie fauna and they drove the flora to a last refuge on railroad embankments and roadsides. To our engineers this flora is merely weeds and brush; they ply it with grader and mower. Through processes of plant succession predictable by any botanist, the prairie garden becomes a refuge for quack grass. After the garden is gone, the highway department employs landscapers to dot the quack with elms, and with artistic clumps of Scotch pine, Japanese barberry, and Spiraea. Conservation Committees, en route to some important convention, whiz by and applaud this zeal for roadside beauty.

Some day we may need this prairie flora not only to look at but to rebuild the wasting soil of prairie farms. Many species may then be missing. We have our hearts in the right place, but we do not yet recognize the small cogs and wheels.

In our attempts to save the bigger cogs and wheels, we are still pretty naïve. A little repentance just before a species goes over the brink is enough to make us feel virtuous. When the species is gone we have a good cry and repeat the performance.

The recent extermination of the grizzly from most of the western stock-raising states is a case in point. Yes, we still have grizzlies in the Yellowstone. But the species is ridden by imported parasites; the rifles wait on every refuge boundary; new dude ranches and new roads constantly shrink the remaining range; every year sees fewer grizzlies on fewer ranges in fewer states. We console ourselves with the comfortable fallacy that a single museum-piece will do, ignoring the clear dictum of history that a species must be saved *in many places* if it is to be saved at all.

The ivory-billed woodpecker, the California condor, and the desert sheep are the next candidates for rescue. The rescues will not be effective until we discard the idea that one sample will do; until we insist on living with our flora and fauna in as many places as possible.

We need knowledge—public awareness—of the small cogs and wheels, but sometimes I think there is something we need even more. It is the thing that *Forest and Stream*, on its editorial masthead, once called 'a refined taste in natural objects.' Have we made any headway in developing 'a refined taste in natural objects'?

In the northern parts of the lake states we have a few wolves left. Each state offers a bounty on wolves. In addition, it may invoke the expert services of the U. S. Fish and Wildlife Service in wolf-control. Yet both this agency and the several conservation commissions complain of an increasing number of localities where there are too many deer for the available feed. Foresters complain of periodic damage from too many rabbits. Why, then, continue the public policy of wolf-extermination? We debate such questions in terms of economics and biology. The mammalogists assert the wolf is the natural check on too many deer. The sportsmen reply they will take care of excess deer. Another decade of argument and there will be no wolves to argue about. One conservation inkpot cancels an-

149

other until the resource is gone. Why? Because the basic question has not been debated at all. The basic question hinges on 'a refined taste in natural objects.' Is a wolfless north woods any north woods at all?

The hawk and owl question seems to me a parallel one. When you band a hundred hawks in fall, twenty are shot and the bands returned during the subsequent year. No four-egged bird on earth can withstand such a kill. Our raptors are on the toboggan.

Science has been trying for a generation to classify hawks and owls into 'good' and 'bad' species, the 'good' being those that do more economic good than harm. It seems to me a mistake to call the issue on economic grounds, even sound ones. The basic issue transcends economics. The basic question is whether a hawkless, owl-less countryside is a livable countryside for Americans with eyes to see and ears to hear. Hawks and owls are a part of the land mechanism. Shall we discard them because they compete with game and poultry? Can we assume that these competitions which we perceive are more important than the co-operations which we do not perceive?

The fish-predator question is likewise parallel. I worked one summer for a club that owns (and cherishes) a delectable trout stream, set in a matrix of virgin forest. There are 30,000 acres of the stuff that dreams are made on. But look more closely and you fail to see what 'a refined taste in natural objects' demands of such a setting. Only once in a great while does a kingfisher rattle his praise of rushing water. Only here and there does an otter-slide on the bank tell the story of pups rollicking in the night. At sunset you may or may not see a heron; the rookery has been shot out. This club is in the throes of a genuine educational process. One faction wants simply more trout; another wants trout plus all the trimmings, and has employed a fish ecologist to find ways and means. Superficially the issue again is 'good' and 'bad' predators, but basically the issue is deeper. Any club privileged to own such a piece of land is morally obligated to keep all its parts, even though it means a few less trout in the creel.

In the lake states we are proud of our forest nurseries, and of the progress we are making in replanting what was once the north woods. But look in these nurseries and you will find no white cedar, no tamarack. Why no cedar? It grows too slowly, the deer eat it, the alders choke it. The prospect of a cedarless north woods does not depress our foresters; cedar has, in effect, been purged on grounds of economic inefficiency. For the

151

same reason beech has been purged from the future forests of the Southeast. To these voluntary expungements of species from our future flora, we must add the involuntary ones arising from the importation of diseases: chestnut, persimmon, white pine. Is it sound economics to regard any plant as a separate entity, to proscribe or encourage it on the grounds of its individual performance? What will be the effect on animal life, on the soil, and on the health of the forest as an organism? Is there not an aesthetic as well as an economic issue? Is there, at bottom, any real distinction between aesthetics and economics? I do not know the answers, but I can see in each of these questions another receding target for conservation.

I had a bird dog named Gus. When Gus couldn't find pheasants he worked up an enthusiasm for Sora rails and meadowlarks. This whipped-up zeal for unsatisfactory substitutes masked his failure to find the real thing. It assuaged his inner frustration.

We conservationists are like that. We set out a generation ago to convince the American landowner to control fire, to grow forests, to manage wildlife. He did not respond very well. We have virtually no forestry, and mighty little range management, game management, wildflower management, pollution control, or erosion control being practiced voluntarily by private landowners. In many instances the abuse of private land is worse than it was before we started. If you don't believe that, watch the strawstacks burn on the Canadian prairies; watch the fertile mud flowing down the Rio Grande; watch the gullies climb the hillsides in the Palouse, in the Ozarks, in the river-breaks of southern Iowa and western Wisconsin.

To assuage our inner frustration over this failure, we have found us a meadowlark. I don't know which dog first caught the scent; I do know that every dog on the field whipped into an enthusiastic backing-point. I did myself. The meadowlark was the idea that if the private landowner won't practice conservation, let's build a bureau to do it for him.

Like the meadowlark, this substitute has its good points. It smells like success. It is satisfactory on poor land which bureaus can buy. The trouble is that it contains no device for preventing good private land from becoming poor public land. There is danger in the assuagement of honest frustration; it helps us forget we have not yet found a pheasant.

I'm afraid the meadowlark is not going to remind us. He is flattered by his sudden importance.

Why is it that conservation is so rarely practiced by those who must extract a living from the land? It is said to boil down, in the last analysis, to economic obstacles. Take forestry as an example: the lumberman says he will crop his timber when stumpage values rise high enough, and when wood substitutes quit underselling him. He said this decades ago. In the interim, stumpage values have gone down, not up; substitutes have increased, not decreased. Forest devastation goes on as before. I admit the reality of this predicament. I suspect that the forces inherent in unguided economic evolution are not all beneficent. Like the forces inside our own bodies, they may become malignant, pathogenic. I believe that many of the economic forces inside the modern body-politic are pathogenic in respect to harmony with land.

What to do? Right now there is a revival of the old idea of legislative compulsion. I fear it's another meadowlark. I think we should seek some organic remedy—something that works from the inside of the economic structure.

We have learned to use our votes and our dollars for conservation. Must we perhaps use our purchasing power also? If exploitation-lumber and forestry-lumber were each labeled as such, would we prefer to buy the conservation product? If the wheat threshed from burning strawstacks could be labeled as such, would we have the courage to ask for conservation-wheat, and pay for it? If pollution-paper could be distinguished from clean paper, would we pay the extra penny? Over-grazing beef vs. range-management beef? Corn from chernozem, not subsoil? Butter from pasture slopes under 20 per cent? Celery from ditchless marshes? Broiled whitefish from five-inch nets? Oranges from unpoisoned groves? A trip to Europe on liners that do not dump their bilgewater? Gasoline from capped wells?

The trouble is that we have developed, along with our skill in the exploitation of land, a prodigious skill in false advertising. I do not want to be told by advertisers what is a conservation product. The only alternative is a consumer-discrimination unthinkably perfect, or else a new batch of bureaus to certify 'this product is clean.' The one we can't hope for, the other we don't want. Thus does conservation in a democracy grow ever bigger, ever farther.

Not all the straws that denote the wind are cause for sadness. There are several that hearten me. In a single decade conservation has become a profession and a career for hundreds of young 'technicians.' Ill-trained, many of them; intellectually tethered by bureaucratic superiors, most of them; but in dead earnest, nearly all of them. I look at these youngsters and believe they are hungry to learn new cogs and wheels, eager to build a better taste in natural objects. They are the first generation of leaders in conservation who ever learned to say, 'I don't know.' After all, one can't be too discouraged about an idea which hundreds of young men believe in and live for.

Another hopeful sign: Conservation research, in a single

decade, has blown its seeds across three continents. Nearly every university from Oxford to Oregon State has established new research or new teaching in some field of conservation. Barriers of language do not prevent the confluence of ideas.

Once poor as a church mouse, American conservation research now dispenses 'federal aid' of several kinds in many ciphers.

These new foci of cerebration are developing not only new facts, which I hope is important, but also a new land philosophy, which I know is important. Our first crop of conservation prophets followed the evangelical pattern; their teachings generated much heat but little light. An entirely new group of thinkers is now emerging. It consists of men who first made a reputation in science, and now seek to interpret the land mechanism in terms any scientist can approve and any layman understand, men like Robert Cushman Murphy, Charles Elton, Fraser Darling. Is it possible that science, once seeking only easier ways to live off the land, is now to seek better ways to live with it?

We shall never achieve harmony with land, any more than we shall achieve justice or liberty for people. In these higher aspirations the important thing is not to achieve, but to strive. It is only in mechanical enterprises that we can expect that early or complete fruition of effort which we call 'success.'

The problem, then, is how to bring about a striving for harmony with land among a people many of whom have forgotten there is any such thing as land, among whom education and culture have become almost synonymous with landlessness. This is the problem of 'conservation education.'

When we say 'striving,' we admit at the outset that the thing we need must grow from within. No striving for an idea was ever injected wholly from without.

When we say 'striving,' I think we imply an effort of the mind as well as a disturbance of the emotions. It is inconceivable to me that we can adjust ourselves to the complexities of the land mechanism without an intense curiosity to understand its workings and an habitual personal study of those workings. The urge to comprehend must precede the urge to reform.

When we say 'striving,' we likewise disqualify at least in part the two vehicles which conservation propagandists have most often used: fear and indignation. He who by a lifetime of observation and reflection has learned much about our maladjustments with land is entitled to fear, and would be something less than honest if he were not indignant. But for teaching the fresh mind, these are outmoded tools. They belong to history.

My own gropings come to a dead end when I try to appraise the profit motive. For a full generation the American conservation movement has been substituting the profit motive for the feat motive, yet it has failed to motivate. We can all see profit in conservation practice, but the profit accrues to society rather than to the individual. This, of course, explains the trend, at this moment, to wish the whole job on the government.

When one considers the prodigious achievements of the profit motive in wrecking land, one hesitates to reject it as a vehicle for restoring land. I incline to believe we have overestimated the scope of the profit motive. Is it profitable for the individual to build a beautiful home? To give his children a higher education? No, it is seldom profitable, yet we do both. These are, in fact, ethical and aesthetic premises which underlie the economic system. Once accepted, economic forces tend to align the smaller details of social organization into harmony with them.

No such ethical and aesthetic premise yet exists for the condition of the land these children must live in. Our children are our signature to the roster of history; our land is merely the place our money was made. There is as yet no social stigma in the possession of a gullied farm, a wrecked forest, or a polluted stream, provided the dividends suffice to send the youngsters to college. Whatever ails the land, the government will fix it.

I think we have here the root of the problem. What conservation education must build is an ethical underpinning for land economics and a universal curiosity to understand the land mechanism. Conservation may then follow.

The Round River

A PARABLE

One of the marvels of early Wisconsin was the Round River, a river that flowed into itself, and thus sped around and around in a never-ending circuit. Paul Bunyan discovered it, and the Bunyan saga tells how he floated many a log down its restless waters.

No one has suspected Paul of speaking in parables, yet in this instance he did. Wisconsin not only *had* a round river, Wisconsin *is* one. The current is the stream of energy which flows out of the soil into plants, thence into animals, thence back into the soil in a never-ending circuit of life. 'Dust unto dust' is a desiccated version of the Round River concept.

We of the genus *Homo* ride the logs that float down the Round River, and by a little judicious 'burling' we have learned to guide their direction and speed. This feat entitles us to the specific appellation *sapiens*. The technique of burling is called economics, the remembering of old routes is called history, the selection of new ones is called statesmanship, the conversation about oncoming riffles and rapids is called politics. Some of the crew aspire to burl not only their own logs, but the whole flotilla as well. This collective bargaining with nature is called national planning.

In our educational system, the biotic continuum is seldom

pictured to us as a stream. From our tenderest years we are fed with facts about the soils, floras, and faunas that comprise the channel of Round River (biology), about their origins in time (geology and evolution), about the technique of exploiting them (agriculture and engineering). But the concept of a current with drouths and freshets, backwaters and bars, is left to inference. To learn the hydrology of the biotic stream we must think at right angles to evolution and examine the collective behavior of biotic materials. This calls for a reversal of specialization; instead of learning more and more about less and less, we must learn more and more about the whole biotic landscape.

Ecology is a science that attempts this feat of thinking in a plane perpendicular to Darwin. Ecology is an infant just learning to talk, and, like other infants, is engrossed with its own coinage of big words. Its working days lie in the future. Ecology is destined to become the lore of Round River, a belated attempt to convert our collective knowledge of biotic materials into a collective wisdom of biotic navigation. This, in the last analysis, is conservation.

The biotic stream is capable of flowing in long or short circuits, rapidly or slowly, uniformly or in spurts, in declining or ascending volume. No one understands these variations, but they probably depend on the composition and arrangement of the soils, faunas, and floras which are the conductors or channels of flow.

A rock decays and forms soil. In the soil grows an oak, which bears an acorn, which feeds a squirrel, which feeds an Indian, who ultimately lays him down to his last sleep in the great tomb of man—to grow another oak:

rock → soil → oak → acorn → squirrel → Indian⌐

Ecology calls this sequence of stages in the transmission of energy a food chain, but it can be more accurately envisioned as a pipe line. It is a fixed route or channel, established by evolution. Each joint in the pipe is adapted to receive from the preceding joint and transmit to the succeeding joint.

The pipe line leaks at every joint. Not all the rock forms soil. Squirrels do not get all the acorns, nor do Indians get all the squirrels; some die and decay and return directly to the soil. Owing to this spillage en route, only part of the energy in any local biota reaches its terminus. This loss of volume may be depicted thus:

rock → soil → oak ↗ acorn ↗ squirrel ↗ Indian

In addition to losses from spillage, energy is side-tracked into branches. Thus the squirrel drops a crumb of his acorn, which feeds a quail, which feeds a horned owl, which feeds a parasite. Thus we see that the pipe line branches like a tree. The owl eats not only quail but also rabbit, which is a link in still another line:

rock → soil ⇕ sumac ⇕ rabbit ⇕ tularemia

Thus we see each animal and each plant is the 'intersection' of many pipe lines; the whole system is cross-connected.

Nor is food the only important thing transmitted from one species to another. The oak grows not only acorns; it grows fuel for the Indian, browse for deer, hollow dens for raccoon, salad for June beetles, shade for ferns and bloodroots. It fashions domiciles for gall wasps; it cradles the tanager's nest; its fallen leaves insulate the soil from frost; its unfallen leaves screen the owl from the crow and the partridge from the fox; and all the while its roots are splitting rocks to make more soil to make more oaks. We see, then, that chains of plants and

animals are not merely 'food chains,' but chains of dependency for a maze of services and competitions, of piracies and co-operations. This maze is complex; no efficiency engineer could blueprint the biotic organization of a single acre. It has grown more complex with time. Paleontology discloses aboriginal chains at first short and simple, growing longer and more complicated with each revolving century of evolution. Round River, then, in geological time, grows ever wider, deeper, and longer.

For the biotic community to survive, its internal processes must balance, else its member-species would disappear. That particular communities *do* survive for long periods is well known: Wisconsin, for example, in 1840 had substantially the same soil, fauna, and flora as at the end of the ice age, i.e. 12,000 years ago. We know this because the bones of its animals and the pollens of its plants are preserved in the peat bogs. The successive strata of peats, with their differing abundance of pollens, even record the weather; thus around 3000 B.C. an abundance of ragweed pollen indicates either a series of drouths, or a great stamping of buffalo, or severe fires on the prairie. These recurring exigencies did not prevent the survival of the 350 kinds of birds, 90 mammals, 150 fishes, 70 reptiles, or the thousands of insects and plants. That all these should survive as an internally balanced community for so many centuries shows an astonishing stability in the original biota. Science cannot explain the mechanisms of stability, but even a layman can see two of its effects: (1) Fertility, when extracted from rocks, circulated through such elaborate food chains that it accumulated as fast as or faster than it washed away. (2) This geological accumulation of soil fertility paralleled the diversification of flora and fauna; stability and diversity were apparently interdependent.

We have dealt, so far, with the characteristics of Round River in the pre-Bunyan eras. What now of that *enfant terrible*, Paul, and we, his heirs and assigns? What are we doing to the river, and what is the river doing to us? Are we burling our log of state with skill, or only with energy?

We have radically modified the biotic stream; we had to. Food chains now begin with corn and alfalfa instead of oaks and bluestem, flow through cows, hogs, and poultry instead of into elk, deer, and grouse, thence into farmers, flappers, and freshmen instead of Indians. That the flow is voluminous you can determine by consulting the telephone directory, or the roster of government agencies. The flow in this biotic stream is probably much greater than in the pre-Bunyan eras, but curiously enough science has never measured this.

Tame animals and plants have no tenacity as links in the new food chain; they are maintained, artificially, by the labor of farmers, aided by tractors and horses, and abetted by a new kind of animal: the Professor of Agriculture. Paul Bunyan's burling was self-taught; now we have a 'pro' standing on the bank giving free instruction.

Each substitution of a tame plant or animal for a wild one, or an artificial waterway for a natural one, is accompanied by a readjustment in the circulating system of the land. We do not understand or foresee these readjustments; we are unconscious of them unless the end effect is bad. Whether it be the President rebuilding Florida for a ship canal, or Farmer Jones rebuilding a Wisconsin meadow for cow pasture, we are too busy with new tinkerings to think of end effects. That so many are painless attests the youth and elasticity of the land organism.

Now to appraise the new order in terms of the two criteria: (1) Does it maintain fertility? (2) Does it maintain a diverse fauna and flora? Soils in the first stages of exploitation display a burst of plant and animal life. The abundant crops that evoked thanksgiving in the pioneers are well known, but there was also a burst of wild plants and animals. A score of imported food-bearing weeds had been added to the native flora, the soil was still rich, and landscape had been diversified by patches of plowland and pasture. The abundance of wildlife reported by the pioneers was in part the response to this diversity.

Such high metabolism is characteristic of new-found lands. It may represent normal circulation, or it may represent the combustion of stored fertility, i.e. biotic fever. One cannot distinguish the fever from normality by asking the biota to bite a thermometer. It can only be told *ex post facto* by the effect on the soil. What was the effect? The answer is written in gullies on a thousand fields and CCC camps on a thousand hills. Crop yields per acre have remained about stationary. The vast technological improvements in farming have only offset the wastage in soil. In some regions, such as the dust bowl, the biotic stream has already shrunk below the point of navigability, and Paul's heirs have moved to California to ferment the grapes of wrath.

As for diversity, what remains of our native fauna and flora remains only because agriculture has not got around to destroying it. The present ideal of agriculture is clean farming; clean farming means a food chain aimed solely at economic profit and purged of all non-conforming links, a sort of *Pax Germanica* of the agricultural world. Diversity, on the other hand, means a food chain aimed to harmonize the wild and the tame in the joint interest of stability, productivity, and beauty.

Clean farming, to be sure, aspires to rebuild the soil, but it employs to this end only imported plants, animals, and fertilizers. It sees no need for the native flora and fauna that built the soil in the first place. Can stability be synthesized out of imported plants and animals? Is fertility that comes in sacks sufficient? These are the questions at issue.

No living man really knows. Testifying for the workability of clean farming is northeastern Europe, where a degree of biotic stability has been retained (except in humans) despite the wholesale artificialization of the landscape.

Testifying for its non-workability are all the other lands where it has ever been tried, including our own, and the tacit evidence of evolution, in which diversity and stability are so closely intertwined as to seem two names for one fact.

One of the penalties of an ecological education is that one lives alone in a world of wounds. Much of the damage inflicted on land is quite invisible to laymen. An ecologist must either harden his shell and make believe that the consequences of science are none of his business, or he must be the doctor who sees the marks of death in a community that believes itself well and does not want to be told otherwise.

The government tells us we need flood control and comes to straighten the creek in our pasture. The engineer on the job tells us the creek is now able to carry off more flood water, but in the process we lost our old willows where the cows switched flies in the noon shade, and where the owl hooted on a winter night. We lost the little marshy spot where our fringed gentians bloomed.

Some engineers are beginning to have a feeling in their bones that the meanderings of a creek not only improve the landscape but are a necessary part of the hydrologic functioning. The ecologist sees clearly that for similar reasons we can get along with less channel improvement on Round River.

Goose Music

Some years ago the game of golf was commonly regarded in this country as a kind of social ornament, a pretty diversion for the idle rich, but hardly worthy of the curiosity, much less of the serious interest, of men of affairs.

Today scores of cities are building municipal golf courses to make golf available to the rank and file of their citizens.

What has happened? Golf has not changed, and certainly golfers have not. The change has been in the public point of view. Golf is no longer regarded as an ornamental sport, but as a valuable means of physical, mental (and, to the golfer, spiritual) recreation. Golf has become a valuable part of our social economy. Of course it has always been valuable to society, but the twentieth century has been the first to realize the fact.

The same change in point of view has occurred toward most other outdoor sports—the frivolities of fifty years ago have become the social necessities of today. But strangely enough, this change is only just beginning to permeate our attitude toward the oldest and most universal of all sports, hunting and fishing.

We have realized dimly, of course, that a day afield was good for the tired businessman. We have also realized that the destruction of wildlife removed the incentive for days afield.

166

But we have not yet learned to express the value of wildlife in terms of social welfare. Some have attempted to justify wildlife conservation in terms of meat, others in terms of personal pleasure, others in terms of cash, still others in the interest of science, education, agriculture, art, public health, and even military preparedness. But few have so far clearly realized and expressed the whole truth, namely, that all these things are but factors in a broad social value, and that wildlife, like golf, is a social asset.

But to those whose hearts are stirred by the sound of whistling wings and quacking mallards, wildlife is something even more than this. Golf is an acquired taste, but the instinct that finds delight in the sight and pursuit of game is bred into the very fiber of the race. Golf is a delightful accomplishment, but the love of hunting is almost a physiological characteristic. A man may not care for golf and still be human, but the man who does not like to see, hunt, photograph, or otherwise outwit birds or animals is hardly normal. He is supercivilized, and I for one do not know how to deal with him. Babes do not tremble when they are shown a golf ball, but I should not like to own the boy whose hair does not lift his hat when he sees his first deer. We are dealing, therefore, with something that lies pretty deep. Some can live without opportunity for the exercise and control of the hunting instinct, just as I suppose some can live without work, play, love, business, or other vital adventure. But in these days we regard such deprivations as unsocial. Opportunity for exercise of all the normal instincts has become to be regarded more and more as an inalienable right. The men who are destroying our wildlife are alienating one of these rights, and doing a terribly thorough job of it. More than that, they are doing a permanent job of it. When the last corner lot is covered with tenements we can still make a playground by tearing them down, but when the last antelope goes by the board, not all the playground associations in Christendom can do aught to replace the loss.

One of the anomalies of wildlife conservation is that our social asset is being destroyed by the very instinct, for the exercise of which we seek to preserve it. I have often wondered why many Americans, decent at home, are such barbarians afield. I think they must be exaggerated 'throwbacks' to the old days when the gentle art of poaching was one of the standard accomplishments of a self-respecting yeoman. If the King still owned all the game, I think I should make a very good poacher myself. I often feel the promptings of the breed. I own I would rather kill a mess of mallards shooting with the *hoi polloi* just outside the gun-club fence than kill a backload on the baited preserve. But the King no longer owns the game. It belongs to my friends and neighbors. The gentle art of poaching, therefore, has assumed a new complexion. The poacher is no longer a hero, but a thief. In time he will come to realize this. It is the duty of the forward-looking citizen to speed the day, and of the law to regulate the poacher's conduct meanwhile.

If wild birds and animals are a social asset, how much of an asset are they? It is easy to say that some of us, afflicted with hereditary hunting fever, cannot live satisfactory lives without them. But this does not establish any comparative value, and in these days it is sometimes necessary to choose between necessities. In short, what is a wild goose worth? As compared with other sources of health and pleasure, what is its value in the common denominator of dollars?

I have a ticket to the symphony. It stood me two iron men. They were well spent, but if I had to choose, I would forgo the experience for the sight of the big gander that sailed honking into my decoys at daybreak this morning. It was bitter cold and I was all thumbs, so I blithely missed him. But miss or no miss, I saw him, I heard the wind whistle through his set wings as he came honking out of the gray west, and I felt him so that even now I tingle at the recollection. I doubt not that this very

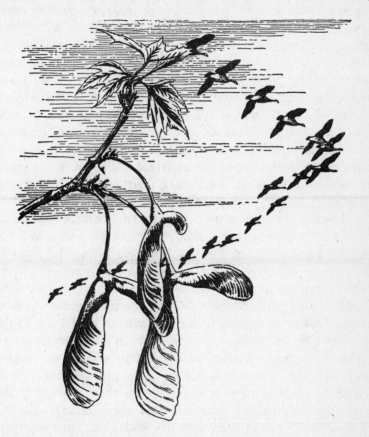

gander has given ten other men two dollars' worth of thrills. Therefore I say he is worth at least twenty dollars to the human race.

My notes tell me I have seen a thousand geese this fall. Every one of these in the course of their epic journey from the arctic to the gulf has on one occasion or another probably served man to the equivalent of twenty dollars. One flock perhaps has thrilled a score of schoolboys, and sent them scurrying home with tales of high adventure. Another, passing overhead of a dark night, has serenaded a whole city with goose music, and awakened who knows what questionings and memories and hopes. A third perhaps has given pause to some farmer at his plow, and brought new thoughts of far lands and journeyings and peoples, where before was only drudgery, barren of any thought at all. I am sure those thousand geese are paying human dividends on a value of twenty dollars each. But the resulting $20,000 is only an exchange value, like the sale value of a painting or the copyright of a poem. What about the replacement value? Supposing there were no longer any painting, or poetry, or goose music? It is a black thought to dwell upon, but it must be answered. In dire necessity somebody might write another *Iliad*, or paint an 'Angelus,' but fashion a goose? 'I, the Lord, will answer them. The hand of the Lord hath done this, and the Holy One of Israel created it.'

Is it impious to weigh goose music and art in the same scales? I think not, because the true hunter is merely a noncreative artist. Who painted the first picture on a bone in the caves of France? A hunter. Who alone in our modern life so thrills to the sight of living beauty that he will endure hunger and thirst and cold to feed his eye upon it? The hunter. Who wrote the great hunter's poem about the sheer wonder of the wind, the hail, and the snow, the stars, the lightnings, and the clouds, the lion, the deer, and the wild goat, the raven, the hawk, and the eagle, and above all the eulogy of the horse? Job, one of the great dramatic artists of all time. Poets sing and hunters scale the mountains primarily for one and the same reason—the thrill to beauty. Critics write and hunters outwit their game primarily for one and the same reason—to reduce that beauty to possession. The differences are largely matters of degree, consciousness, and that sly arbiter of the classification of human activities, language. If, then, we can live without goose music, we may as well do away with stars, or sunsets, or *Iliads*. But the point is that we would be fools to do away with any of them.

What value has wildlife from the standpoint of morals and religion? I heard of a boy once who was brought up an atheist. He changed his mind when he saw that there were a hundred-odd species of warblers, each bedecked like to the rainbow, and each performing yearly sundry thousands of miles of migration about which scientists wrote wisely but did not understand. No 'fortuitous concourse of elements' working blindly through any number of millions of years could quite account for why warblers are so beautiful. No mechanistic theory, even bolstered by mutations, has ever quite answered for the colors of the cerulean warbler, or the vespers of the woodthrush, or the swansong, or—goose music. I dare say this boy's convictions would be harder to shake than those of many inductive theologians. There are yet many boys to be born who, like Isaiah, 'may see, and know, and consider, and understand together, that the hand of the Lord hath done this.' But where shall they see, and know, and consider? In museums?

What is the effect of hunting and fishing on character as compared with other outdoor sports? I have already pointed out that the desire lies deeper, that its source is a matter of instinct as well as of competition. A son of a Robinson Crusoe, having never seen a tennis racket, might get along nicely without one, but he would be pretty sure to hunt or fish whether or not he were taught to do so. But this does not establish any superiority as to subjective benefits. Which helps the more to build a man? This question (like the one we used to debate in school about whether boys or girls are the best scholars) might

171

be argued till doomsday. I shall not attempt it. But there are two points about hunting that deserve special emphasis. One is that the ethics of sportsmanship is not a fixed code, but must be formulated and practiced by the individual, with no referee but the Almighty. The other is that hunting generally involves the handling of dogs and horses, and the lack of this experience is one of the most serious defects of our gasoline-driven civilization. There was much truth in the old idea that any man ignorant of dogs and horses was not a gentleman. In the West the abuse of horses is still a universal blackball. This rule of thumb was adopted in the cow country long before 'character analysis' was invented and, for all we know, may yet outlive it.

But after all, it is poor business to prove that one good thing is better than another. The point is that some six or eight millions of Americans like to hunt and fish, that the hunting fever is endemic in the race, that the race is benefited by any incentive to get out into the open, and is being injured by the destruction of the incentive in this case. To combat this destruction is therefore a social issue.

The difficulty, however, is not so much in proving this principle in the abstract as in getting people to see and respect its applications. I have seen many a women's club pass resolutions on bird protection, but the 'aigrettes' do not come off. I have seen many a law-abiding citizen sit down to a banquet of illegal quail-on-toast, and loudly proclaim his sportsmanship or patriotism. Many of the 'best people' at our summer resorts unblushingly buy trout or grouse or venison, and feel delightfully wicked about it, because they see nothing broken but a law. Members of the 'Four Hundred' in a Middle Western town I know openly flout the spring-shooting regulations, and their friends accept with warm thanks the ducks thus stolen from their sons. Nightingales' tongues were doubtless merely meat

172

to Nero, but it is about time to expect enlightened Americans to know and do better than he.

To conclude: I have congenital hunting fever and three sons. As little tots, they spent their time playing with my decoys and scouring vacant lots with wooden guns. I hope to leave them good health, an education, and possibly even a competence. But what are they going to do with these things if there be no more deer in the hills, and no more quail in the coverts? No more snipe whistling in the meadow, no more piping of widgeons and chattering of teal as darkness covers the marshes; no more whistling of swift wings when the morning star pales in the east! And when the dawn-wind stirs through the ancient cottonwoods, and the gray light steals down from the hills over the old river sliding softly past its wide brown sandbars—what if there be no more goose music?